Introduction: About

I t would be challenging to find their histories, mindsets and ap point. George Campbell and Jim rackard personify the two very different groups of the population that this book explores. The fact that they have been able to understand each other and work together is a testament to the underlying promise of "The Consistency Chain for Network Marketing."

<u>As George Campbell explains...</u>

My high school yearbook from Enid, Okla., didn't have cute predictions about graduating seniors. But if it did, mine would have been, "Great potential!" This is a nice way of saying, "Hmmm, we had hoped you would do better." How do I know that? Because year after year, teacher after teacher would just shake their heads at me in despair, "Why won't you just apply yourself?!"

Post-college, I jumped from job to job. I tried my hand at network marketing opportunities. I fell in love with the time and freedom promises of this elegant business model. I attended all the trainings. I was a loyal customer of the product. I was in awe of the top producers and vowed I would model their actions and "walk across the stage." But it never happened.

I internalized as much frustration and shame as I was capable of holding. Then I did what millions of other aspiring distributors do.

I quit.

Fortunately, I found stand-up comedy. I had a natural ability, little fear of the stage, and the 23 and ½ hours of daily free time fit perfectly into my schedule. I was a constantly booked, solid performer who (for reasons that will become clear) never made the jump to fame or big money.

My years of stand-up comedy prepared me to shift into the world of professional speaking. Again, I repeated my pattern of solid performance with rare spurts of excellence. Those random moments happened just often enough to torture me. "Why can't I muster that level of consistent effort and performance all the time?"

That question was the underlying mystery of my life. I had one real asset in trying to unravel this riddle: I never blamed my failure on anyone else. As painful as the truth was, I accepted the ownership of my struggles. As Walt Kelly once wrote, "We've met the enemy, and he is us."

The power of this brutal self-awareness is that if you believe you are the cause of your problems, you understand that you can be the solution. I never stopped looking for that "magic bullet" that would fix me. Despite decades of disappointment, I never gave up hope.

This book is the culmination of that search. The answer is as unlikely as the person who made the connection. To be blunt, I am a professional business humorist who combined the theories of an 18th century Italian philosopher with an idea from a world-famous comedian. And in that absurd smash-up, I found the answer to my lifelong under-performance.

For the first time in my life, I feel certainty, where before there was doubt. Here is the statement I can now make with pride: "I can now make a promise to myself and feel certain I will keep it."

I have won over my greatest enemy (myself) and made him my ally. Our goal is to help you do the same.

And from Jim Packard...

I first met George several years ago. We were both involved in the same network marketing opportunity. I was "Distributor of the Year." George was firmly holding down the other end of the bell curve. Despite our respective positions, we became friends. As a leader, George represents all those sharp capable people who were a puzzle to me. By all rights, they should be absolutely soaring, yet I was unable to get them off the ground.

When George shared with me how he wanted to offer a solution to the underachieving 80% of the population, I was really intrigued. I realized how many people we could possibly impact and what that would mean to all of us. As someone who had built traditional businesses and network marketing organizations with thousands of distributors and customers, I had experienced first-hand the frustration of trying to help people who were seemingly beyond my assistance.

The question I asked George was, "Why do you need me? You could do this without me." What I came to understand is we are wired very differently. While George speaks directly to the 80% experience, I am able to provide the 20% counterpoint. My hope is that I can empower the 20% high-performers to better understand and assist their consistency-challenged associates.

There is one confession I need to share. In the areas of business, income and family, I have enjoyed great success. (Against my natural reluctance, George is going to make me share some of that. He says it's about establishing credibility. To me, it feels a lot like bragging.)

There is, however, a part of my life over which I have never gained control. That is my health. In this area, I am undertaking the same journey that we are urging for our readers. The thought of developing power and mastery in this sphere of my life is every bit as exciting as the other successes I've enjoyed.

I grew up in a small town in Maine. As kids, my friends and I would play baseball from morning until dusk, breaking only for lunch and dinner. On occasion, we would be missing a friend or two because they took the day off to go to the country club beach.

I remember the feeling that I had as I watched my good buddies drive away with their parents. They would wave as they headed to the lake (in their convertibles, no less). The country club had a strict visitors' policy. A guest could go but only once a month. I cherished my monthly visit and dreaded the 30-day wait for the next one. I knew someday I was going to become a member, so I could go anytime I wanted to.

As I grew older, I noticed all of my friends' dads owned different businesses. Robby's dad owned a furniture store, Terry's dad owned a Buick dealership, and Jimmy's dad owned a bunch of buildings. I decided early on that business ownership was the key to the country club—and the convertible that would drive me there. I could visualize myself as an entrepreneur. I could see myself as a member of that country club. That was my first sense of exposure to having a dream and the power of delayed gratification.

I didn't use the phrase "delayed gratification" when I was young. I simply had the innate ability to set big goals and work hard until I obtained them. Time and again, I demonstrated this goal-oriented behavior.

As a fourth-grader selling greeting cards for Lincoln Elementary School, I won the prize I desperately wanted: a white pearl-handled knife. The victory was only slightly tainted by the fact that I sliced my finger on the bus ride home. I never saw the knife again. The prize may have been gone, but the pattern was firmly set.

When I was a little older and had a paper route, the "Miami News" sponsored a big contest. The top-three people in new subscribers would win a trip to the Seattle World's Fair. Places four through 60 got to attend a New York Yankees baseball game. I was a big Mickey Mantle fan and was determined to win that prize. I overshot. I came in first. So I used my keen negotiating skills, trading places with the kid who came in fourth.

After working my way through college, I started a company with $500. I had a goal of building a successful business and being able to retire by age 50. Thirty days before that birthday, I sold my business to a Fortune 500 company and retired.

Maybe I should define what retired looked like for me. My first "retirement" hobby was to team up with a very talented inventor. We took a couple of products from concept to marketplace. I especially enjoyed appearing on QVC over 25 times, selling millions of dollars of products.

Then I rekindled my interest in network marketing. I became "Distributor of the Year" in two different companies. I came to love this business model and appreciate the people who were willing to attempt it.

If all this sounds like bragging, don't blame me. George made me do it. And the point of it all is that I enjoyed a great deal of success.

I had the ability to set and realize goals. I also came to understand a great number of people seemed incapable of doing what I had done. Whether they were the salesmen in my copier business or the distributors in my network marketing organizations, there was a deep disconnect between what worked for me and didn't work for them.

I counseled frustrated distributors. I shared the systems and methods that drove my success. Then I would see them struggle and fail with them. I did not understand the gulf in our respective thinking. I did not understand we were literally "wired differently." I do now.

With that new understanding, I have tremendous excitement about helping people in a way that is right for them.

Chapter 1

Vilfredo Pareto

In the late 1800s, an Italian scientist, theologian and philosopher observed a phenomenon in the distribution of wealth in Italy. He found that the bulk of the riches were owned by a minority of the people, and the minority of wealth was held by most of the people. As his research continued, he soon realized this formula had much broader application. His theory, which became known as the "Pareto Principle," held that 80% of outcome is derived from 20% of all input.

For example:

- 20% of seeds planted will result in 80% of the total crop.
- 20% of customers will generate 80% of revenue.
- 20% of a sales force will account for 80% of the sales.

George—*For 20 years, I performed a program for corporate events. I created the character "Joe Malarkey, The Worst Motivational Speaker in America." It was a spoof of all the tried and true ideas, philosophies and platitudes of traditional keynote speakers. It succeeded beyond my expectations, mainly because it was the right program at the right time.*

That's why, 10 years into that stretch, I was shocked by a phone call I received. A prospective client was interviewing me to see if

Joe Malarkey might be the right speaker for their event. As best as my memory can reconstruct the exchange, here's what he said, "George, we are a classic Pareto Principle company. Eighty percent of our sales come from 20% of our salespeople. Twenty percent of our sales come from 80% of our salespeople." Then he asked me a question that still amazes me to this day. "How can what YOU do help us reverse this situation?"

Remember, he is calling <u>ME</u>, Joe Malarkey—The <u>Worst</u> Motivational Speaker in America—to fix this problem. That can only mean one thing. He has called everyone else in the directory! If his job depended on coming up with a solution, he had two things on his to-do list that day:

- *Call this Malarkey guy.*

- *Update his resume and start looking for new employment.*

When he asked me how I could help, immediately three things came to mind. First, Pareto's Principle is a law. So, I don't know that what you want to do is even legal. Second, if it is legal, I don't know if it is possible. And third, if it is legal and possible, I have absolutely no idea how I would help you.

That's what I thought. What I said was, "I think I can help you!" (Right, like you've never lied to try to get work.) Despite my counterfeit confidence, he quickly recognized quickly I had no solutions.

That conversation occurred more than 10 years ago. I never forgot it. And of note, if anything, the 80/20 Rule today may be more pervasive and proven than in years past.

For years, people have studied this Pareto phenomenon. Research has been compiled and books have been written. Without exception, the approach in analyzing and understanding it has been consistently "Top Down." People have traditionally investigated this principle from the corporate or organizational point of view.

- How can we get our people to focus on those high-leverage 20% actions that generate 80% results?
- How can we attract the 20% of clients that generate 80% of our income?
- How can we hire the 20% performers who will produce 80% of our revenue?

What has been largely unexplored is this "bottom up" question:

- What could account for this wide gap between the high producing 20% and the lesser performing 80%?
- Once identified, how can we help the 80% enjoy more success?

To dismiss this mystery is to accept that four out of five people are going to spend their entire lives underachieving. On one hand, businesses spend hundreds of thousands of dollars trying to develop their "Corporate Culture," and on the other hand their only plan for dealing with their "80% performers" is to ignore or replace them.

Jim—I recently had a conversation with a top income earner from a network marketing company and commented on how many good people leave our profession. I was expecting to hear, "Yes, we need to do a better job at retaining those people." But instead he said, "We'll just have to find new people!" No wonder this industry has such a tarnished reputation. And, no wonder leaders face burnout from this perpetual recruiting treadmill.

In my traditional business experience, I knew that the cost of hiring a new employee was much greater than the expense of keeping a current employee. In network marketing, we emphasize the acquisition of a new distributor much more than the retention and advancement of a current one. If someone doesn't get connected and stay connected, we just seem to let them go quietly in the night. Imagine the benefits to both the companies and the individuals if a fraction of those people stayed the course.

As I mentioned earlier, I built and sold a business to a Fortune 500 company. The first five people we hired were with us when we sold the business 22 years later. That continuity drove the growth that made our company such an attractive acquisition.

Setting aside the bottom-line cost of employee or distributor turnover, what about the personal price paid by the 80%? These are not "bad" people. They are simply performing below their potential.

The first step to assisting this vast majority is to understand the real cause of their underperformance. To isolate that, you first must eliminate characteristics common to both the 20% and 80% groups:

- Intelligence
- Education
- Talent
- Ability
- Motivation
- Skills
- Training
- Even ambition

These are all traits we associate with success and performance. Yet, they are equally present in both camps. So, what is the one overriding differentiator?

Consistency.

Put simply, the 20%-ers do what needs to be done, when it needs to be done **consistently.**

The 80%-ers know what needs to be done, know how to do it, but their efforts are hit-or-miss, erratic and irregular.

Inconsistent.

What has been the time-tested method of dealing with this disparity in performance? On a regular basis, meetings are held. People sit in the audience as person after person speaks to them from the stage. Who are these presenters? They are company leaders, outside speakers, experts and gurus. And what do all these presenters have in common? They are all 20%-ers. Their high-level 20% performance is what granted them the right to be on that stage.

They will share the "20%" ideas, techniques and philosophies that have worked for them. And that information will resonate with exactly 20% of the audience. Meanwhile, the 80%—the people we are desperate to impact—will go away unfed. How do we know this approach has been ineffective? Simple. The numbers don't change.

It's not because the 80% don't understand the information—they do. But the greatest ideas in the world will not work for the 80% because they won't apply them consistently. This is not an intelligence or knowledge problem. *This is a consistency problem.*

Until this underlying issue is addressed, the other stuff is a waste of time. It doesn't matter how many great strategies, plans and ideas you introduce if 80% of the group won't employ them consistently. Imagine a company that would repeatedly roll out a software upgrade, knowing in advance, it would crash four out of five computers. That would never happen. And yet companies and organizations are willing to do exactly that with the most valuable asset they possess: their people.

However, if you can successfully solve the consistency problem, then those 20% ideas are like rocket fuel.

George—*The reason why I was fascinated by the "bottom up" view of this problem is very simple. My entire existence has been spent observing life from that angle. I am a card-carrying, dyed-in-the-wool, head-to-toe 80%-er. Consistency has been the biggest challenge in every area of my life.*

That doesn't mean I haven't enjoyed occasional success. I have. Just not consistent success.

I've spoken to hundreds of audiences, been interviewed on "60 Minutes," and featured on the front page of the "LA Times." (Jim didn't have to ask me to brag, it just comes naturally). If I'm an 80%-er, how was that possible?

Simple: I am an 80%-er who is capable of an occasional hard sprint. Every accomplishment listed above is due to one spurt of action. I generated enough momentum during that surge that I was able to coast for the next 15 years. And that is exactly what I did. I can sprint. But the second that I stop, I drop. I fall right back to my inconsistent 80% ways with the same 80% results.

I will never forget the night I was inducted into the National Speakers Association's "Speaker Hall of Fame." My introducer was reciting my accomplishments. As she was ticking off the list, I realized the man she was describing was not in the room. The person who had done all those things had not existed for two years. I understood completely how it feels to have "imposter syndrome." The "George Campbell" who earned that award was gone. The most I could do was accept on his behalf.

The reason I was so interested in solving the 80% inconsistency issue is not because I wanted to save the world. I just wanted to save myself. And I did. I don't know if this can save the rest of the world. I do believe it can save you.

Jim—*In my years of traditional business experience, I had witnessed the Pareto Principle. I had hard numbers that showed 20% of my sales reps accounted for 80% of our company's sales. It became more glaring once I entered the network marketing world. As a leader, it was particularly frustrating because I didn't understand why people couldn't follow the proven game plan that worked for me. Not until George and I started working together did I realize one size doesn't fit all.*

One really important point needs to be emphasized. We are not viewing the 80% from a position of judgement or condescension. We don't believe the 80% are in any way "less than." Nor do we believe the 80% are in some way defective or broken.

They don't need to be fixed.

We simply believe (and will scientifically prove) they are wired differently. The solution for them is going to be dramatically different than the methods that work for the 20%.

It is past time for the 80% to stop blaming themselves for failing with methods that were never meant for them. It is time to commit to a new approach, specifically designed for the 80% wiring. It's time to start winning.

Consistently.

Chapter 2
The 'Churn'

Eric Worre, a prominent writer, speaker and consultant in the MLM world defines success in network marketing this way: **"Getting a large number of people to do a few simple things on a consistent basis."** This formula obviously has validity beyond just the world of direct sales.

There are three components to this formula:

"Getting a large number of people...."

This is recruiting and hiring. Companies and individual distributors spend a great deal of time, energy and effort in this area.

"...a few simple things...."

This is training. Again, a major point of emphasis. It is a rare company that does not have well-developed training materials. They are everywhere. Online, offline, in meetings, through events, and with one-on-one training and coaching.

"...on a consistent basis."

This is the final piece. This is where organizations and leaders make a fatal mistake. They assume if they recruit or hire good people and train them well, those people are going to be consistent. Nothing could be further from the truth. That is why the single biggest lament of leadership is, "I can't get my people to do anything!"

If anything, the lack of consistency is more pervasive in network marketing than it is in other professions. As an employee in a traditional business, poor performance is always accompanied by the threat of being fired.

That doesn't exist in network marketing.

The MLM accountability model (if it can even be called that) is literally "all carrot and no stick." And for the 80%, "all carrot" is not enough to overcome their natural tendency to be inconsistent. Separated from the external structure and punishment-enforced expectations of a job, the 80% are ill prepared to generate the self-discipline necessary for consistency and eventual success

By focusing on just two of the three factors of Eric Worre's formula, it's very difficult to build a self-sustaining organization and business. In effect, we keep producing two-legged stools. Then we're amazed when they're unstable and won't support our weight.

The Pareto Principle is present in all businesses. But, the nature of network marketing makes it one of the most dramatic examples of the 80/20 divide. Because of its "volunteer" structure, it is akin to a time-lapse view of a traditional business.

The hiring process in a traditional business is long and thorough. It generally takes a significant amount of time and a great deal of evaluation before a person is hired. That is also reflected in the exit process. Because of the litigious environment, very rarely is someone fired. And just as infrequently does someone leave of their own volition. It does happen. But it occurs at a much slower pace. In network marketing, the turnover is rapid and constant.

George—*To join many companies, there are only two questions you have to answer correctly: Do you have a checkbook and do you have it with you?*

Jim—*We have standards. They're low, but we have them.*

Another factor in the constant tide of distributors is the low initial investment. Compared to launching a traditional business, joining a network marketing venture is a much easier financial decision. Unfortunately, what is very easy to start is also equally easy to quit. If a person doesn't experience success and experience it quickly, they are gone. Who are these people who come and go constantly? They are the 80%.

They become "The Churn." They are the great mass of people who join a company, muster only inconsistent effort and receive inconsequential rewards. Over a period of weeks or months, they simply melt away. Then they are replaced by others, just like them, who will follow the same trajectory.

Jim—*Most network marketing events are like Broadway shows. The people on stage rarely change, but the audience is different every time.*

In network marketing, these inconsistent, disappointed people in the audience don't just disappear. Instead they become part of this ever-growing mass of "lack of success" stories. "The Churn" is the 800-pound gorilla that network marketing companies would prefer to ignore. Unfortunately, when it runs out of bananas or gets bored with its tire swing, that gorilla is capable of strolling over and crushing them.

George—*I had the poor judgment of engaging in a conversation about network marketing with a person who had very strong opinions. Now understand, he wasn't personally involved with a company. In fact, he had never been a part of any company.*

That did not stop him from condemning the entire industry. He told me only a tiny percentage of people make it. And if they do, they are just profiting off the gullibility and foolishness of the people who don't.

Where does this uninformed, yet strident opinion come from? "The Churn." This is not a rare point of view. We can disagree with it. We can try to refute it. What we can't afford to do is ignore it.

This black cloud of failure is a drag on individual companies and the entire industry. The undertow of negative experiences is what feeds and nourishes the less than positive perception of network marketing. It is not a large leap from "network marketing didn't work for me" to "network marketing doesn't work."

There are many who dismiss "The Churn" as just the cost of doing business. Their strategy is to cast a wide net, "sort for leaders," and toss the rest back into the ocean. There certainly is a basis of logic in this. After all, leaders lead. Leaders recruit. Leaders are consistent. Leaders are 20%-ers. And if you are a 20% leader, wouldn't you want to surround yourself with people just like you?

We are not suggesting the pursuit of leaders should end. We are suggesting a significant portion of the great mass of "non-performers" can be helped. Many can grow into the role of "leader." But that is rarely going to happen using the methods that have been traditionally employed.

Jim—*There's an old saying, "You don't know what you don't know." Regardless of what business I was in, I always had the same sledgehammer approach to increasing sales. If I wanted to improve the numbers, I would rely on myself (and a few others) to go out and get it done. That was my exclusive focus. If I had taken the time to become a better leader and not always tried to put a square peg in a round hole—oh, how much better could we have been?*

It serves no purpose for a leader to complain, "I can't get my people to do anything!" That statement is not helpful in finding a solution. Let's pose a more useful question, "How can I help inconsistent people to be more consistent?" A phrase often heard is "You can't push a rope." True. But what if you could gently pull it?

"The Churn" is network marketing's biggest challenge and greatest opportunity. What if there existed a strategy to enable a significant portion of the 80%-ers to develop a level of consistent performance? Setting aside the benefit for the company, imagine the difference it could make in the lives of all those people who were swayed by the promise of "You can do this!" or "You were made for this business!"

Jim—An adage in network marketing is, "Your future lies in people you haven't met yet." That couldn't be truer. Most of the top performers who came into my organization were people who I certainly didn't know. Most of them came in at the fifth or sixth level. If you're a leader, think of the most productive people in your organization and ask yourself, "Did I personally recruit this person?"

The answer is usually no.

From a personal standpoint, I got lucky. I was sponsored by one of the giants in our industry. He didn't know me from Adam. A person who wasn't even in his business referred me to him. Once I expressed some interest in the opportunity, the person who referred me was given the chance to be my sponsor. He declined. (Bad decision.) My personal team included three of the company's top-10 income earners for years.

A friend of mine made the following statement that resonated with me. He said, "Not everyone is a prospect. But everyone is a resource for you." I've tried to keep that in mind not only when I meet someone new but also with everyone who has joined our team. I treat them as a valued asset, regardless of their success. I'm not sure if there's a bigger compliment in the business world than having someone say, I want to join your team.

Quick aside, George, did I ever tell you how I got into the MLM business to begin with?

I received a letter in the mail that said, "Your name has come to our attention as the type of person who possesses the talents and skills that we're looking for. We would like to invite you and your wife to join us Thursday evening at 7:00 at the Holiday Inn downtown Hartford to explore an opportunity that matches your abilities and skills" (or something to that effect).

I'm thinking, "YES! Finally, someone recognizes my talents! They must have heard that I just won the company trip to Bermuda!" Our store G Fox and Company awarded me a trip for two as the manager with the highest percentage over quota. It hadn't been reported in the newspaper, but obviously the word of my stellar performance must have gotten out.

In reality, the invitation was a form letter sent out to 1,000 people. I later found out that of all those recipients, I was the only one to respond to that letter. And because of that action, thousands of people have positively benefited. How crazy is that?!

Not as crazy as spending a tremendous amount of time, money and energy to attract people into a business. And then do nothing as they silently leave.

Chapter 3
Pure and Partial

I f you're a 20%-er, here is a question you might be asking: "This book isn't about me. Why should I be reading it?" There are two answers to that question.

If you're a 20%-er, there is a very good chance that you are in a leadership position. If that is the case, odds are that a high percentage of the people on your team are 80%-ers. How many? While the authors of this book do not possess higher degrees in math, we're going to go out on a limb and say, "About four out of five."

The relationship dynamic of a 20%-er trying to coach an 80%-er can be a frustrating experience for both. What seems incredibly easy for the coach appears unattainable for the student. All the techniques, strategies, programs and tactics that work fabulously for the 20%-er are wasted on the 80%-er. Not because they don't work. They're wasted because the 80%-er will not implement them **consistently**.

If this bedrock issue is not addressed and overcome, neither party is going to be as successful as their potential promises. So, the answer to the question, "Why should I (the 20%-er) read this book?" is so that you can help your 80% people achieve real progress and growth.

Jim—*Just realizing there's a strategy to help the 80%-ers is like a breath of fresh air. It's so frustrating to feel like you have the answers and yet are not able to impact the people in your business. Simply providing the "How to" is not enough. Getting people to grasp your ideas and suggestions is just the first step. If they won't take action consistently, the subsequent efforts are wasted.*

Out of sheer frustration, you will hear leaders say, "We want it more for them than they want it for themselves." What I've come to learn is that is not true. It is not a question of "want to" or even "how to." It is a question of finding a method for the naturally inconsistent to become consistent.

As part of the 20-percent group, it's imperative that we recognize that not all people are wired the same. It was only after I started to look at myself in the area that I'm an 80%-er (remember, health issues and weight control?) did it dawn on me that my general approach has been all wrong in trying to reach the 80% group.

Let me explain: As an entrepreneur, I created a customized point system that has been developed and refined over the last 40 years. The system has helped me build multiple businesses. It's a system that most 20%-ers love. It's got everything: a goal setting formula, action plans and a reward system. The daily worksheet has accountability built all through it and has been adopted by many companies.

Now, here is what has been a real eye opener for me in my conversations with George. I realized I needed to approach my weight loss in an altogether different way. My elaborate point system that worked perfectly in other parts of my life failed me completely in this area. Frankly, I should have come to that realization on my own. Instead, I blamed myself for this failure, rather than questioning the approach that I was using.

This mirrors perfectly the real-world results of foisting 20% strategies on 80% people. When they fail, we blame the people, rather than the strategy.

I've finally realized that in the area of health and weight, I am an 80%-er. I am naturally inclined to be inconsistent. I need to approach my health in a different way. In the same way, I need to use a different method with 80% of my team members.

The second reason this book should be of interest to 20%-ers is simple. As Jim just shared, there are very few pure 20%-ers. A perfect example of this is Oprah Winfrey. Is she a 20% businesswoman? No doubt. She built an empire in one of the most competitive fields on earth. She established herself in the culture to the point that she is recognized by just her first name.

Is she a pure 20%-er? No. In the area of health, fitness and weight control, she is in the fight just like any other 80%-er. This is true despite all the advantages that her wealth provides. She can afford private chefs, personal trainers and access to the finest workout facilities. She could easily hire someone whose entire job would be to do nothing but follow her around and slap the food out of her mouth. And yet she struggles with consistency.

The two facets of her mindset were demonstrated when she decided to join Weight Watchers. Before the announcement, the 20% business side of her purchased a large block of Weight Watcher stock. She knew that the instant her decision was announced that the stock would shoot up. Which it did. How she will fare in her latest attempt to conquer weight loss and maintenance (the 80% area of her life) remains to be seen.

Examples of partial 20%-ers abound. We all know top performers who are superstars in their career and failures in their relationships. They make all the money in the world and have a home life that none of us would care to live. The opposite is also true. We know the person who is barely eking by on the job. Making quota is always a race to the last day of the month. And that same person is a model spouse and parent.

When it comes to consistency, there are very few of us who are "pure" across every area of our life. So, for the 20%-er trying to find the relevance of this material, we ask, "Is there an area of your life that resists improvement?" If there is, the technique we're going to suggest could help you finally power through that last barrier to a whole, integrated life.

George—*While there are few examples of "pure" 20%-ers, I have the misfortune of having one of them as my best friend. Maybe this was God's way of preparing me to co-write this book. Or maybe I am being paid back for something awful I did in a previous life. I'm leaning toward the second explanation.*

The contrast between my buddy and I could not be sharper. If he is going to do something, he is going to do it on time and at a high level. If I am going to do something, I am going to do it late, poorly and then slack off from there.

He is a scratch golfer. I am an itch golfer.

As a young man, he was a male model. As a young man, I couldn't even build a model.

While going to college, he had two majors, worked full time and bought a house. While I was enrolled in college (notice I didn't say "attended"), I came in fourth in my fraternity's Foosball tournament. He graduated Summa Cum Laude. I graduated, "Hey, where's the party?!"

I'm kidding. I didn't graduate.

The point is, there are a few pure 20%-ers out there. And there should be a bounty on them.

Chapter 4

Hope

You should be prepared for the next chapter of the book, "The Marshmallow Test." It is a little discouraging. Even depressing. Before you tackle it, let's share some critical hope over the next few pages.

George—I'm not kidding around when I say that I'm an 80%-er. I failed at five different network marketing opportunities. In addition, I've have had one traditional business venture succeed, one flounder and four outright crash. I have six years of college under my belt and am still 53 hours short of getting a degree. (I like to think I'm in the 74th semester of my sophomore year.) If you look up 80% in the dictionary, it should have my photo. But it won't, because I didn't show up to have my picture taken.

If you're a discouraged 80%-er, I am right by your side. I understand the frustration and shame that comes from knowing what I want to do and not being able to get myself to do it. Consistently. I have always felt like I could do more, be more and have more. And just couldn't get myself to <u>do</u> more.

Sound familiar?

You are going to be presented with a solution. Not some theory that sounds good. A real solution designed for the 80%. We have a plan specially structured for people who have a tough time following a plan. How do I know it will work for you? Because I did it first. I had to prove to myself that there was something that would actually work. For me, George, "80% poster child."

In August 2016, I happened across what we call, "The 800 Million Dollar Idea." At first, I didn't really consider it. In fact, it took an entire month before I decided to give it a try. (Did I mention that I'm an 80%-er?) I finally gave it a shot. After all, I had failed at so many things—what's one more?

I decided I would attempt to get control over one part of my life: my health. Now I wasn't in terrible shape but according to the BMI chart, I was borderline obese. I could play 18 holes of golf. With a cart. And a nap. Also, I avoided public pools that allowed harpoons.

I made the decision that I was going to get in better shape. I was going to be stronger, healthier and more fit. I was going to work out for 45 minutes, during which I would elevate my heart rate and sweat.

And I was going to do it EVERY DAY.

Now understand, other than eat, I can't think of anything I have ever done EVERY DAY. It was a ridiculous project. A 20%-er would have a tough time. For an 80%-er, it was a pipe dream. I told absolutely nobody. It's bad enough to fail; I saw no reason to broadcast it.

September 24, 2016, I went to the gym. September 25th, I poured my aching body into the car and went to the gym again. In fact, I made it to the gym all the rest of September.

And October.

And November.

And December.

In mid-January, I got the flu. I didn't miss a day. Month after month, I experienced a level of consistency that was new, empowering and exciting.

September 24, 2017 was day 365. Not a single day was missed. Not one. I don't tell you this so you will think I'm amazing. I tell you this because I'M AMAZED!!!

On the heels of this newfound consistency, I leveraged my momentum into a second area of my life. And it is working there, also.

There is nothing in my personal history that would suggest that this could happen. So, if you are reading this, know one thing: there is hope.

It is real. It is possible. It is simple.

You can do this.

Jim—*I'm so excited to think that I finally have a strategy that I can lose some weight and get healthy. I've found something that's not overwhelming. I can focus on one task, like walking three miles every day.*

I started on Friday the 13th, which is scary enough but as each day passes, I get more and more confident that I can make it work this time. I'm not going to lie to you—I am tempted to add another exercise or two. A lot of my well-meaning friends know that I'm on a quest to lose weight. They have offered many helpful tips, like eat with my left hand, eat slowly, use smaller plates, eliminate carbs, watch videos on health, join a Facebook group, read a book, get a trainer, track my progress, etc., etc., etc. Just listing all of these tips puts me into total confusion and paralysis.

In the past, I would have considered all the opinions. I would have weighed and evaluated each approach, ranked my options, scheduled my activities. I would have assigned points and rewards based on difficulty and benefit. And then I would have done the same thing I have always done in this area of my life:

Nothing.

This new approach has produced results I have never experienced in the past. I have been at this for less time than George, but I have now walked over 256 days. (I allow myself about two rest days a month.) Although I have been tempted, I have avoided making all the charts and forms of my typical point and reward system.

I'm experiencing a confidence I've never felt before. I used to try to find ways to avoid exercising, but now I seem to power through those challenges. It's fun, empowering and rewarding to see "I am Healthier," "I am Fitter" on my calendar.

And if that isn't enough good news, I've already experienced additional unexpected benefits. I usually do my three-mile walk early in the day. Once I'm done, I feel like I've taken one giant step toward my most important goal. Building on that feeling of accomplishment, a "prospecting" call becomes much easier. As Jim Rohn said, "Every discipline affects every other discipline."

Although I'm not where I want to be yet, I feel good about myself and I'm heading in the right direction. My doctor took note of this at my last check-up. As he charted my lower weight and much improved blood pressure, he asked me, "What the heck are you doing? "

I gave him this book.

Chapter 5
The Marshmallow Test

Beginning in 1960, a Stanford researcher named Walter Mischel conducted a study. He began by rounding up a group of 300 5-year-old children.

Mischel sat across the table from each child and presented them with an option. He set a single marshmallow on the table. Then he said, "I'm going to leave the room for 15 minutes. You are free to eat the marshmallow—but, if you don't, when I return, I will give you a second marshmallow."

Then he left.

Any guesses on the percentage of kids who were able to fight off the impulse to eat the marshmallow? You nailed it: 20%. And the other 80% were overwhelmed by their desire for immediate gratification. Some kids ate the marshmallow before Mischel had even gotten out of the door.

Pause and think for second. Try to put yourself back into the 5-year-old "you." Would you have eaten the marshmallow?

George–*Absolutely. There is not a doubt in my mind. How can I be so sure? Simple. I'm a grown man who cannot be trusted to keep cookies in his house. A package of Oreos has a life expectancy of an insect in a fly-swatter factory. If Oreos were animals, PETA would picket my house. So, if a cookie is more powerful than me* *as a grown man, what kind of resistance would I have had as a 5-year-old marshmallow eater?*

Jim–*I would have waited for the person to come back into the room, so I could receive another marshmallow. I think I would have viewed it as a challenge, and challenges have always motivated me.*

George–*Of course Jim wouldn't have eaten the marshmallow. In fact, I'm guessing Jim still has the first marshmallow he ever earned. To appreciate the difference between us, you only have to look at our college experience.*

Jim–*I worked full-time and graduated in four years. Getting my college degree was a hard-won challenge. I lived in a different place every semester. Parent's house, grandmother's house, sister's house, boarding house, a house with five guys, dormitory, fraternity house and finally an apartment with my bride. Talk about delayed gratification!*

George—*The only shared experience here is that I also joined a fraternity. I went with the frat that had a permanent beer keg in the living room and an unobstructed view of the Chi-O house.*

Back to the Marshmallow Test. If the study had stopped there, it would have been interesting. But it did not. Years later, they realized they had enough contact information to track down the participants. The kids, now 17-18 years old, were surveyed. Was there a difference? Yes. A dramatic one. The teenagers who did not eat the marshmallow had higher GPAs, higher SAT scores, and were judged to be more socially advanced.

Twenty years passed, and another follow-up study was undertaken. Now nearly 40-years-old, the non-marshmallow eaters were found to possess lower divorce rates, have a better sense of self-worth, pursued their goals more effectively, and had greater health as measured by a lower body-mass index. In virtually every metric, the 20% far surpassed their marshmallow-eating brethren.

In the meantime, medicine, science and technology had made giant leaps. In 2011, the "kids" now in their 50s, were examined one last time. Using a fMRI machine, a technician was able to look at the activity level in two areas of the subject's brain and predict with complete accuracy whether that person ate the marshmallow 50 years prior.

For the non-marshmallow eaters, the seat of most decision making is in the prefrontal cortex. This is frequently referred to as the "executive" functioning center of the brain. It is here that we evaluate immediate actions in the context of probable long-term results. When this part of the brain is in charge, we have the ability to think at a "higher level." We can make the prospecting call, knowing it will possibly lead to building our dream business. We can introduce our product to someone, knowing it will bring value to them and profit to us. We can pass up the donut, knowing that doing so will likely lead to a healthier body. We can put down the cell phone and actually engage in conversation with our spouse, knowing that it will likely lead to a more satisfying relationship.

For the marshmallow eaters, the story is dramatically different. The decision to scarf down the marshmallow is formulated in the ventral striatum. This part of the brain evaluates action (or non-action) based on completely different criteria. It asks these questions based on E.S.P. Is it Easy, is it Safe, and is it Pleasurable? In other words, what is the IMMEDIATE impact of this decision? For a few millennia, these were great questions:

- Easy? Am I going to expend more calories pursuing this food source than I'm going to get in return?

- Safe? Am I going to proceed with alertness and caution, or is a tiger going to be using my femur as a toothpick?

- Pleasurable? Am I going to enjoy the pleasure of procreation, thus assuring the future of my species?

Your long line of ancestors answered these questions correctly. Otherwise it would be somebody else reading this book. However, in our current world where food is easy, life is relatively safe, and pleasure is everywhere, these guidelines no longer serve us well.

When modern-day decisions are reduced to these factors, the results are sadly predictable.

- Reach out to a prospect or don't reach out?
- Hop on the leadership call or watch TV?
- Stay in bed or drive to the gym?
- Save for the new iPad or whip out the credit card?

George—*And the winner is…The Ventral Striatum! If I had a tattoo, it would read: "Well, it seemed like a good idea at the time."*

The first step to understanding *why* we make some of the decisions we do is to understand *where* we make some of the decisions that we do. In the context of this fundamental difference between the 20% and the 80%, the conclusions that can be drawn from the Marshmallow Test are sobering:

1) The ability to delay gratification is perhaps the major determiner of how successful we are going to be in virtually every part of our lives.

2) That ability is hardwired into us by at least the age of five and maybe earlier.

For the 20%, this is great news. You have won the pre-adolescent lottery! For the rest of us, we are apparently working off some very bad past-life karma. We have received the equivalent of a slow death sentence to our dreams of achievement.

If that doesn't terrify every 80%-er out there, then you need to re-read this chapter.

Imagine telling a 5-year-old, "Honey, you ate the marshmallow. So, for the rest of your life, you will never experience the joy and satisfaction that comes from reaching lofty goals." Can you fathom saying those words to a 5-year-old?

Jim–*Hold on a second. Now we both know that I'm not great with technology, but...*

George–*My partner has a gift for understatement. Jim has trouble downloading bread out of a toaster.*

Jim–*...and yet, I managed to Google the "Marshmallow Test." Its findings are kind of controversial.*

True. The initial test has been much criticized. Most of the "debunking" focuses on one major flaw. The children sampled were all part of the Stanford University community. They were all members of the middle to upper middle class. The impact of this narrow sampling becomes apparent in the subsequent studies.

A multitude of researchers have tried to replicate the findings of the Stanford study. Their results show that the economic level of the subject has an overwhelming influence on whether or not they eat the marshmallow. Unsurprisingly, when faced with an uncertain future, people in poverty overwhelmingly opt for the "sure thing" of immediate reward. As one writer put it, poverty can cause people to live in the "permanent now."

Critics therefore contend that whether a 5-year-old ate a marshmallow is a much less reliable predictor of their future success than the subject's impoverished or advantaged economic status. But before we start throwing out babies and bathwater, let's consider the two critical things the researchers do agree on:

- Instant gratification, whether driven by poverty or other factors, greatly diminishes the likelihood of favorable long-term outcomes.

- As indicated by the fMRI tests, the seat of this desire resides in the ventral striatum.

The problem revealed by Mischel is unchanged. How do people, whether poor or well-off, change "immediate gratification" behaviors? For anyone wrestling for control of their life, the question of "How did I get here?" is much less important than "How can I change this?"

Whether it is the high-potential distributor struggling to build a profitable business, or the impoverished child choosing between TV time or study time, the solution is the same.

Like most behavioral issues, the first step of the solution is to acknowledge its existence.

Carl Jung, the founder of humanistic psychology said, "It is a paradox, but we must first accept ourselves as we are, then we change."

The 80% are left with three options to accomplish this critical change in orientation:

1) Learn to delay gratification (not possible—already tried that and failed)...

2) Give up (lower the expectations for your life), or...

3) Use, repurpose and leverage that innate desire for instant gratification to achieve long-term goals.

To accomplish this third approach, we encourage the reader to "give in" to this urge for immediate fulfillment. But, do it in such a way that it actually takes them closer to the "delayed gratification" objective that they desire. This is going to require a new way to judge our daily successes.

One thing all professional network marketers can agree on is that this business model is NOT a "Get Rich Quick" scheme. It can take months and years of consistent effort to build a vibrant and growing business. And during that journey, the signs of progress can be difficult if not impossible to see. The consistency-challenged 80% need a measurement system that allows them to feel pleasure in the immediate win and still make progress toward a distant reward.

Lastly, keep in mind two things. Number one, our book is focused on helping the reader develop the skill of consistency. Yet, this entire chapter has constantly referred to delayed vs. instant gratification. The reason for this is simple: Delayed gratification and consistency are inseparable. Consistent action is the how delayed gratification manifests in the real world. Delayed gratification is a mental construct. Consistent action is the outward reflection of that idea. A similar example would be "charity" is a mental state, "giving" is the physical expression. Scientists have a name for delayed gratification without consistent action to support it. They call it instant gratification.

Number two, we live in a competitive and comparative world. It is easy to look at high achievers and feel shame, to feel less than. Maybe you haven't performed at a level that you know you're capable of doing. That doesn't mean that there is something wrong with you.

You're not broken.

You've simply been handed the wrong owner's manual. It's like trying to operate the dishwasher with the instructions for the blender. No matter how many times you press "Puree," the dishes don't get clean. And what is our natural reaction to this failure? Do we question the owner's manual? No. We kick the dishwasher.

Not anymore.

Sexy cartoon character Jessica Rabbit said, "I'm not bad. I'm just drawn that way." The same draw of nature applies to the 80%. They are not bad. Not lazy, unmotivated or character flawed. *They are different.* And the way to success is going to be very different.

The first step to creating a new user's manual for the 80% is to throw out one of the all-time, gold-standard, highly touted, oft-recommended, motivational speaker exalted principles.

And we're going to commit this act of blasphemy in the next chapter.

Chapter 6
George Clooney and 'ER' Goals

G oals don't work. Let's be more specific. Goals and goal setting don't work for the 80%.

Upon examination, this makes perfect sense. What is a goal? It is something we don't currently possess; it is unattainable at the moment. We are separated from our goal in both distance and the time it will take to reach it. A goal is the very embodiment of delayed gratification.

What do we know about the 80% and their capacity to delay gratification? They suck at it. No wonder they struggle with attaining long-term goals. Given the fact that they couldn't wait 15 minutes for a marshmallow, what are the odds of them toiling for weeks or years for a reward that is distant, difficult and uncertain?

George–The first time I heard about SMART goals I got very excited. You see, we 80%-ers totally understand all the stuff that works for the 20%-ers. We just can't do it consistently. SMART goals were a perfect example of this. SMART is an acronym that stands for: Specific... Measurable... Assignable... R (I never can Remember)... and Time-based.

First of all, think how excited the guys were when the letters lined up that way. It could have just as easily been MARTS or TRAMS. Neither one of which is nearly as cool.

I got so excited. At the time, I weighed 205 quivering pounds. I immediately set a SMART goal. "I, George (assignable) will weigh 175 pounds (specific and measurable) by Jan 1, 2011 (time based)." This is a textbook perfect SMART goal. (Except for the "R", which I still can't remember.)

You can imagine the joy and pride that I felt as I stepped on the scales that January 1, 2011. There I was, still hung-over from a New Year's Eve party. I stared down between my woozy toes. (That's right, even my feet were hung-over.) The number spun up on the scale: 205! Why, in six short months I had gone from an out-of-shape, lethargic 205-pound slob to a SMART goal-setting, highly motivated, 205-pound slug. Talk about consistency!

Some speakers urge the concept of BHAGs—Big, Hairy, Audacious Goals. (What is it with motivational speakers and acronyms?) This is the poster child of 20% ideas. BHAGs are designed to inspire, motivate and incite action. The theory is that we need to think big! Think impossible! Think so outrageously wild that we will fly into action!

That might work for the 20%. For the 80%, it accomplishes just the opposite. We cut out the picture of the mansion, the Rolls Royce and the Porsche, the yacht and the island. We paste them on some poster board. We stare at them and smile. Until our 80% brain kicks in and the smile fades.

George—*Here's a real-world example of how a BHAG can freeze the 80%. I was working with a network marketing company. The upline leader held a weekly conference call. One week, he announced a promotion/contest. The winner would receive a fabulous prize. There were a few hundred people on that phone call. Because the reward was big and the number of people vying for the prize would be large, each listener evaluated the chances* *of their winning to be zero. So, what did they do? Absolutely nothing.*

The next week, the winner was announced. Actually, the winner was not announced. Why? Because NOBODY did anything! We 80% were so sure we couldn't win that we did NOTHING. So, as a leader, when you introduce the big goal and nothing happens, it's not because the 80% don't believe you. It's because they don't believe themselves. More specifically, they don't believe "in" themselves.

<u>Jim</u>—*I was first formally introduced to goals and goal-setting by a friend of mine in my first corporate job out of college. We were both working late one night at a retail store. It wasn't busy, so he told me to take a break and read a book. I didn't have any books in my office, so he gave me one called "Think and Grow Rich" by Napoleon Hill.*

After reading that book, I wrote down 22 things I wanted to own. I just needed a vehicle to fund those items. That search led me to my first MLM company. (By the way, I still have my original set of goals matted and framed on my wall.)

That initial exercise has led me to a system of goal-setting that has served me well over the years. I developed a program that incorporates yearly, monthly and daily goals. It is a work of art that any 20%-er would be proud of! It has timetables, action plans, and reward systems that are fun, are challenging and make me accountable.

The thing I'm most proud about is the impact goals have had on my kids. I remember vividly when my boys came to me while in junior high school and asked me what I wanted for Christmas. They had earned some money from doing their chores and wanted to buy me something. I didn't want them to spend their money on me. I told them that the best gift they could ever give me was their goals in writing.

We selected three areas at that time:

- *Sports (What team do you want to make?)*
- *Family (Be nice to your Mom, Dad, brother and dog)*
- *Academics (My wife, Sherry, insisted on academics, probably due to her Valedictorian background).*

We set one goal in each area, came up with two action plans for each goal, and a reward they were to receive if they accomplished either their goal and/or action plans. It was the same form that I used building my business and still use today.

Every year, my kids gave me their goals in writing. This continued through their college graduations. Those written goals mean more to me than any award I've ever received. My kids have always been light years ahead of other kids their age, and I'm convinced that our goal-setting exercise played a big part of that. (That along with my wife's genes!)

George–*I know what would have happened if my Dad told me that all he wanted for Christmas from me was my written goals. He would have gotten a tie. Or soap-on-a-rope. I tended to alternate each year.*

Goal-setting can be tremendously effective for the 20%. But, if traditional goals aren't effective for the 80%, what can they do? First, we need to understand that the 80% can't change their essential nature. They are always going to be driven by our overpowering urge for immediate gratification. The answer is this: Don't fight immediate gratification. Use it.

To do this, we have to make some fundamental adjustments in the way we view goals and long-term progressive success. We can't just put the picture on the refrigerator and believe that is somehow going to pull us through the finish line. For the 80%, the only thing the law of attraction has attracted so far is frustration and inconsistency.

Here is the change we are going to make. We are not going to set goals. We are going to establish directions. In doing so, we are going to harness the power and instant gratification of "ER."

George–*I used to love to annoy my wife when she was watching George Clooney's breakout hit, "ER". I'd come in the room and say, "What's on? Is that Urrrr? That hospital show, Urrrr? Is that George Clowney? Is that Urrrr?" (It's difficult to imagine why that marriage didn't work out.)*

An "ER" goal is very different from all the traditional goal-setting that has failed the 80%. Traditional goals have very specific metrics we want to attain and usually a timeline or deadline attached. By that reasoning, an "ER" goal isn't really a goal at all. In fact, we are better served to think of "ER" as setting a direction.

"ER" goals are simple words that end in "er." BettER, wealthiER, healthiER. And if "ER" becomes too unwieldy, you can also describe the direction in terms of "more." More rank advancement, more earnings, more time spent with the people important to me.

George–*Instead of setting a traditional goal to get in shape (I will weigh 175 pounds by January 1!), my "ER" goal (direction) was simply "I will be healthiER, strongER, fittER." And I firmly believed that after every single workout, I hit my goal. I was in fact healthier, stronger and fitter. And because of that, I was instantly gratified. There was no distant, unattainable dream over the horizon. There was simply a high-leverage activity that was taking me in the direction that I wanted to go. Every day felt great and complete in itself. Every day was a marshmallow.*

***Jim**–For the 20% who swear by SMART goals, I have a refinement. With the goal-setting approach I have used for years, I actually have a "SMARTER" formula. I added the "E" which stands for "Excuses." (List all of the things that could keep you from reaching your goals.) The "R" stands for rewards. (What are you going to reward yourself with if you reach your goal?) To be clear, my system is exactly what we don't suggest for the 80%.*

"ER" goals are a stark contrast to the SMART (or Jim's SMARTER) process. The achievement/reward model of traditional goals is deemphasized in "ER" goals. This is because there is no well-defined finish line to this "ER" journey. Just like there is no end to a direction. For example:

- Traditional goal: I will work out every day for a year.

When is the goal realized? In 365 days. What are the odds that any card-carrying 80%-er will reach that 365 mark? Just short of none. Traditional goals ask us to hold focus on the big picture, regardless of how distant and daunting it is. "ER" goals simply ask us to take a daily step in the direction that we desire.

- "ER" goal: I will be fitter, healthier and stronger. I will work out just today.

***George**–In 2014, I had a goal to workout 300 days in one calendar year. On January 3, I hurt my foot and that was the end of that goal. In reality, that goal ended on January 1st because I never really believed I would attain it. The pressure of 300 workouts was too much. So, at the first opportunity, I found an excuse to abandon the effort.*

With my "ER" direction, it was never my goal to work out every day for a year. Based on my history, that would have been completely unrealistic. Instead, I only focused on my daily action.

And, until a health challenge put me into bed, that string of "daily victories" extended for 531 consecutive days.

There is another benefit to setting a direction. As you proceed further along the path you have chosen, what had been traditional goals now become mile-markers along the way. They aren't "finish lines" they are just indicators of the progress made.

This is an important distinction because when a goal is set, there are two possible outcomes:

1. You miss it (disappointing)

2. You hit it (gratifying, but dangerous)

For instance, let's say you set a goal to lose weight. You hit your goal. What happens next? The stories are legendary of people who have hit a weight loss goal and in a matter of months gained it all back. Plus a few extra pounds. (This is why you don't see a "Biggest Loser" reunion show. The results would be too depressing.)

After hitting a goal, there are basically two options: Setting another goal or committing to a program of maintenance.

For the 80%-ers, neither of these options are attractive. For 80%-ers to deny their basic instant gratification nature and attain a goal is nearly impossible. To ask them to turn around and do it again and again is unrealistic. We call it "Goal Fatigue." This happens frequently in sales organizations.

Picture the middling performer, who for some crazy reason decides the current sales contest or incentive trip is his for the winning. Against all odds and personal history, he blitzes ahead. All distractions are ignored. He works longer and harder than he ever has. To everyone's surprise, he wins! In fact, not only does he win the trip, he wins something else. Upon his return, tanned and happy, he is given his second prize: a higher quota. Now he is faced with a new, more challenging target. All the energy and excitement of the first race is gone. Welcome to "goal fatigue."

In network marketing, there are many examples of a distributor "hitting a level" once and being unable to reach it again. They use all their energy on achieving the goal and have nothing left to support it. Contrast that with an entire group simply doing their high-leverage activities consistently. That growth is organic and sustainable.

The other option is maintenance. It would be difficult to imagine a less attractive, more energy-sucking goal than maintenance. Oral Roberts was an evangelist who built a sprawling, futuristic university in Tulsa, Okla. He was constantly building and enlarging. There always was a fundraising drive for the new arena, new library or new hospital. A reporter once asked him when this would end. Will this university ever be done? Oral Roberts just laughed. He said, "It's easy to raise money for the new building. Do you know what is hard for people to get excited about? Donating money for the water bill."

It is much easier to lose weight than it is to maintain the weight loss. It is easier to save money than to keep it. It's easier to attain a rank in network marketing than preserve that ongoing level of production. With an "ER" goal, you are not maintaining. You are celebrating a fresh victory every single day.

Now a case can be made that this is just a trick, a mind game. *Of course it's a mind game!* Where did we think this game would take place? The 80% have been playing a mind game for their entire lives.

What this strategy offers is a way to play that game and win for the first time.

Consistently.

Chapter 7
Navy SEALS

Hollywood provides a constant flow of comic book superhero movies. We are besieged on a weekly basis by a new crop of crimson-caped, tights-wearing, computer-graphics-enabled, photoshopped faux Supermen and Wonder Women.

All this, while real heroes go largely unheralded. These are the heroes who don't have the option of calling for a stunt double. This would be more of an insult if those real-life heroes actually desired the spotlight. The men I'm referring to are those members of our elite military special forces. During World War II, Winston Churchill acknowledged them with his words, "We sleep safely at night because rough men stand ready to visit violence on those who would harm us." These words have only become more accurate with each passing year.

In the United States, these are the men of the Joint Special Operations Command. That group is comprised of the Army's Delta Force and Rangers, the Air Force Special Tactics Squadron, and the unit that has drawn the most attention recently, the Navy SEALS. Since the Bin Laden raid, it is rare that anyone is not familiar with SEAL Team 6.

Our appreciation of this last group can only grow as we learn more about the long, arduous process they survive to join the SEAL teams. And "survive" is exactly the right word.

Two things are important to understand at the outset.

1) These are all volunteers. Nobody taps you on the shoulder and forces you to be a Navy SEAL.

2) Not just any sailor in the fleet even gets the opportunity to try out.

You have to pass a battery of exams: medical, aptitude, psychological and, finally, physical fitness. That last test requires the candidate to swim 500 yards in under 12½ minutes, perform 50 push-ups in two minutes, 50 sit-ups in two minutes, 10 pull-ups in two minutes and finally end with a mile and a half run in under ten and a half minutes. All these fitness trials follow one after the other, with a minimum of recovery time. Each candidate is motivated, capable and highly fit.

And 80% of them will fail.

George–*The SEALs provide a great example of how the Pareto Principle is a fractal. You can divide and subdivide a group but in each segment, the ratio remains the same. For instance, out of the entire Navy, only a small group can even qualify to try out for the SEALs. They are the 20%. But once there, 80% of that group will quit.*

And you would think that once you became a SEAL, that's where it would stop. No. Once in the teams, the top 20% will be selected for SEAL Team 6. And I'm sure if you were to ask, you would find that in SEAL Team 6, they could name the top 20% of that group. But then, they would have to kill you.

The qualifying course is called BUD/S: Basic Underwater Demolition/SEAL training. It is a six-month course administered at Coronado Island, California. It is divided into three phases. The first is the shortest, called Indoc. This phase is where 80% of the candidates will opt to leave. Not dismissed. Not sent back to the fleet against their will. Four out of five of these highly motivated, supremely fit candidates will suddenly decide that being a Navy SEAL is no longer their dream.

While the five-week Indoc course is called "training", there is very little actual instruction involved. Instead, active Navy SEAL instructors are trying to find those who are worthy of joining them in the teams. Or perhaps more accurately, they are seeking to eliminate all those who are not equipped to be SEALs.

Each day begins before dawn on a slab of concrete called "The Grinder." Here, the men will do push-ups, sit-ups, leg lifts, pull-ups and dips to the point of exhaustion. All the while being sprayed with cold water from hoses and yelled at continuously from their instructors. The Indoc phase is sometimes called "four weeks and one long day."

The "one long day" is actually Hell Week. It begins late Sunday night and runs until Saturday. The first "day" is 36 hours of continuous stress and unrelenting exercises. The candidates will have the opportunity for just three and a half hours of sleep during the entire week. Of those who make it to this "one long day," half will quit during Hell Week.

So why is the design of this course so diabolically hard and what are the attributes they are screening for? It really boils down to just one. They want SEALs who, under the direst conditions, refuse to quit. It doesn't matter how cold, miserable, hurt, sleep-deprived, exhausted or wounded the candidate is, he refuses to quit. And the only way they can determine who possesses this quality is to push each candidate to and through their breaking point.

And why is this so prized a quality? To understand this is to understand how the SEALs actually deploy and fight. They are sent into treacherous situations in very small groups. At times, their team may only contain four men. In an army of 10,000, if one man quits, it won't even be noticed. In a squad of four, one man's surrender to the pain may be the difference between life and death for everyone.

In the movie "Lone Survivor," a four-man SEAL team is surrounded and attacked by over 200 Taliban fighters. One of the men suffers four wounds, any one of which would be fatal. And he refuses to give up. Or in the SEAL vernacular, he is "always in the fight." He refused to acknowledge his condition. His thinking was, "I can't be dead, I have ammunition left." As long as that was the case, he was in the fight. He is the reason his teammate, Marcus Luttrell, was able to survive, escape and finally tell his story.

The purpose of the first phase of BUD/S is to simulate, as close as possible, the extreme conditions that SEALs will be forced to perform and persevere through. Each SEAL has to know two things: The SEAL beside him will never quit, and he will never quit on the SEAL beside him.

Recently, the Navy made an adjustment to the first phase of BUD/S. In response to the increased use of special force operators around the globe, the Navy wanted more candidates in the pipeline. They cut the first phase of BUD/S from five weeks to three weeks.

An amazing result occurred. Shortening the course by two weeks made absolutely no difference. At three weeks, 80% of the candidates still failed. Under examination, the reason becomes obvious. Those who were going to make it through five weeks were going to make it through three weeks. And those who couldn't survive five weeks weren't going to survive three weeks.

Simply put, it's not the difficulty of the task that determines the success rate. It is the mindset of the participants. The candidates who went on to become Navy SEALs had a different mental approach than all the candidates who washed out.

It is difficult to research those who failed, because they're not asked to write books and or do interviews. But, by studying those who succeed, it is easy to reverse-engineer the difference in thinking. The contrast is subtle and powerful. And it is one we can apply daily in pursuit of consistency and in our desire to build our businesses.

Here is the thinking of the candidate who is not going to make it. It is pre-dawn, and he is on The Grinder. He is cold, soaking wet, and already exhausted. His arms are shaking as he tries to maintain the push-up position. His muscles are still sore and aching from the preceding day. He is, in a word, miserable. And the thoughts begin, "I have five weeks of this. FIVE weeks! I don't see how anybody can do this for five weeks! I don't think I can do this for five weeks. In fact, I know I can't do this for five weeks. I'm not going to make it. And if I'm not going to make it, I might as well quit now. There is no point in putting myself through this agony for another day or another hour. I might as well quit now. I quit."

And with that downward mental spiral, the candidate stands to his feet. He walks across the Grinder, rings the bell, places his helmet on the ground. By the end of Phase One, there will be well over 150 helmets in a row. They represent the long line of candidates who gave up on their dream and walked away.

Contrast that with the mindset of the eventual SEAL winners—one that can be verified because it is a thought process outlined in numerous books and interviews. This candidate is suffering exactly the same amount of pain as the other. His thinking starts exactly as the other candidate. "I have five weeks of this. FIVE weeks! I don't see how anybody can do this for five weeks! I don't think I can do this for five weeks. In fact, I know I can't do this for five weeks."

And then he redirects his thoughts. "I can't do this for five weeks. BUT... I *can* make it to breakfast. And at breakfast, I'll get a rest. I'll eat something. I'll get warm. Five weeks is impossible, but I can make it to breakfast."

He has a goal: becoming a Navy SEAL.

But the thought of surviving those five weeks is too daunting. The goal and reward are too distant. If he concentrates on that, it will actually demotivate and disempower him. Instead, he refocuses his thinking on an activity that he believes he can accomplish. Just make it to breakfast.

And after breakfast, what's the goal?

Make it to lunch.

The afternoon is so long, the thought of making it to dinner is too distant. Now, his goal is simply to make it to the end of whatever evolution of exercises he is currently performing. When he makes it through that day and wakes up the next, what is his goal? Just make it to breakfast. If he just makes it to breakfast, day after day, then at some point he will stand at attention, and his superiors will pin the Navy SEAL Trident on his chest.

In the same way, we can have a very ambitious direction. But for the 80%, we have to attain it through consistent activity. That activity must be believable. It is not required that we believe we will ever reach our distant goal. We just have to believe that we can do this day's activity.

Let's say you've been told that in order to build a successful network marketing business, you'll need to personally talk to a thousand people. (This is a completely made-up number). For the 80%, that knowledge would immediately start throwing up E.S.P. (easy, safe, pleasurable) roadblocks.

- How long would that even take?

- What would I say to 1,000 people?

- How many of them are going to say "No," reject me, or even laugh at me?

- I don't even KNOW 1,000 people!

Instead of that, how about we just "make it to breakfast?" Forget 1,000 people. Take that off the table. Ask yourself this, "Could I talk to one person today?"

If you have managed to read this far in the book, we know you could talk to one person. More importantly, you know it, too.

But what about tomorrow? Will you be able to do it again tomorrow?

Do you want the short answer?

No.

Chapter 8
The Big Lie

If we were going to list all the reasons for 80% failure, this would top the list: The myth of "tomorrow."

The concept of tomorrow is without a doubt the single biggest stumbling block to consistency. It allows 80%-ers to accept failure in a way that seems acceptable. It is very palatable to say, "I'll do that tomorrow." That sounds much better than, "I'm never going to do that."

Tomorrow is that ever-receding mirage. It is the day when all the lights are going to be green. It is the day when we finally have all the necessary time, money, energy, support, knowledge and courage. It is the day when we are finally going to show the world just exactly what we are made of!

And it never arrives.

Let's examine the concept of tomorrow. As an exercise, put down the book for a few seconds. Focus. Concentrate. And then...

Do something tomorrow!

Nope? Nothing happened? Don't feel bad. In the history of man, no one has ever done anything tomorrow. The concept of tomorrow is one of the biggest stumbling blocks of the 80%-er. For 80%-ers, tomorrow is where dreams go to die.

George—*How did I amass 531 consecutive workouts? Simple. I just worked out today. That's it. In fact, if you ask me if I'm going to work out tomorrow, I would tell you, "No." That's because, in the entire streak, I've never worked out tomorrow. Just today. That's the only day that I ever had to win. Like my Navy SEAL role models, I just made it to breakfast.*

I never felt any pressure about what I was going to do in the future. I never gave any thought to "tomorrow." Using that "only today" mindset, I reached a level of consistency that I never dreamed possible.

Jim—*I've always believed in setting goals, but the secret to my success has been in taking daily action.*

Tomorrow doesn't exist. Take the weight of tomorrow off your back. Today is the only day we have to act. Today is the only day we have to succeed. We just have to win today. There is absolutely no pressure to maintain our consistency because we aren't worried about tomorrow. Just today.

We just have to make it to breakfast. Today.

Jim—*As you might expect, coming from New England, I am a big Patriots fan. I watched the 2017 Super Bowl in amazement. No team in Super Bowl history has ever come back from a 10-point deficit. And the Patriots were down by 25 points in the second half. The Falcons had a 99.6% win-probability with 4:40 left in the 4th quarter.*

So how does a team overcome those odds? How do the Patriots in the final eight minutes and 49 seconds go from having less than a 1% win-probability to even odds at the end of regulation?

Six Patriots players were wired with microphones. Afterwards, I could listen to their in-game encouragement and urging. It was a drumbeat of "One play at a time, one play at a time. Focus, Focus,

Focus." They expressed no concern about what happened in the disastrous first half. They didn't worry about what was going to happen at the end of the game. They maintained relentless concentration on the "Now."

And, in case you don't remember, they won the game.

George—*Even more impressive, they did all that with a deflated football.*

Jim—*Here's another tip: Never ever let your partner have the last edit of a book.*

If you want to give yourself a dose of reality, here's some good medicine. When you are tempted to defer action, do this: Instead of saying, "I'll do it tomorrow," say "I am never going to do that. Never."

- I am *never* going to build a business.
- I am *never* going to call a prospect.
- I am *never* going to be more skilled.
- I am *never* going to be healthy.
- I am *never* going to build a better relationship with my spouse or child.
- I am *never* going to be more knowledgeable.

Are you comfortable with those statements? Maybe they are a little harsh. A little fatalistic. Here's what else they are. They are honest.

Jim—*There was always a mystery surrounding the sales contests I had in my traditional businesses and the 30-day challenges and 90-day blitzes I conducted over the years in network marketing. I never understood why the same people always won and the majority of the team never fully participated.*

Now I get it.

For the inconsistently inclined employees or team members, 30 or 60 days is an eternity. They simply don't believe they can perform a challenging action consistently for that span of time. And because they don't believe, they don't participate. They may "whoop it up" when the contest is announced and applaud the winners when it is over, but nothing in their daily activity changes.

Challenges and blitzes are fun, but you have to accept the fact the majority of your team aren't going to be a part of the race. The approach to help them is radically different. It has to be believable. And it has to be about today.

Just today.

Don't buy into the lie of tomorrow. Today is all we have. Today is all we are ever going to have. Fortunately, today is the only day that we are required to win.

Chapter 9

Motivation vs. Momentum

Motivation holds an exalted place in our culture. Network marketing leaders are constantly asking the question, "How can I motivate my distributors?" Parents question, "How can I motivate my kids?" Coaches look for new and unique ways to motivate their teams.

Very rarely does anyone take the time to really think about this mystical thing, "Motivation."

George—Let me go on the record, I'm not against motivation. I have very good friends who are top motivational speakers. I respect what they do and love being in their audiences. I can't imagine anyone not enjoying that feeling of energy that they provide.

Here's the problem. When I fly (which is a great deal), I will inevitably be drawn into a conversation with a seatmate. At some point, the question will be asked of me, "And what do you do?" Here I have a choice. I can lie and introduce a guaranteed conversation stopper, "Why, I sell life insurance to people I meet on planes!" Or I can say, "I am a professional speaker." The response to this question is always the same, "Oh, like a motivational speaker?" This is always delivered with a condescending half-smile and a look of pity. The unsaid message is, "Oh, what a shame you couldn't find a real career."

This is a puzzle. If motivation is something everyone wants, why would there be such a lack of respect for someone who could theoretically provide it? The answer to that lies in the limited power of motivation and our personal experiences with it.

The key to understanding motivation is defining what it is and acknowledging its inherent limitations. Motivation is a feeling. And like any other mental state, it is temporary and fragile. It is subject to all the winds and whims of the world.

We have all witnessed the super-motivated person. The one who is standing on his chair chanting, "I will until!" The person vibrating so much they make coffee jittery. The person who is absolutely unstoppable. Until they stop.

What happened? Life happened. A person said, "No." A distributor quit. A prospect declined to join. The car broke down. The stock market had a hiccup. The promotion went to someone else. The kid ate the dog's homework. Something happened. That's pretty much the definition of life: One after another, things happen. Some good, some bad, some tragic, some exciting. Event after event occurs, each one having an impact on how we feel and our level of motivation.

We are all familiar with the idea that nothing is good or bad. It is strictly our reaction that makes it so. In other words, it is not what happens to us, but how we choose to respond. This is certainly the ideal personal philosophy. This is a view of life to which we all should aspire.

But we also have to concede that virtually no one is able to do this all of the time. This depersonalizing of events requires tremendous mental strength and extremely consistent (there's that word again) mental discipline. If 80%-ers had that kind of control over our thoughts and emotions, delayed gratification would be a piece of cake.

For an 80%-er, it is naïve to believe that a positive motivational state can survive these constant assaults from the world. Imagine holding a spoon, filled to the brim with nitroglycerin. Your goal is to not spill a drop. It would require constant attention, controlled breathing and steady hands.

Now, imagine this same challenge—on a roller coaster. That is the 80%-ers impossible task of trying to hold onto a "motivated feeling" when facing the up and down onslaught of a highly volatile world.

What are the options when we get the "motivational wind" knocked out of us? The one recovery method most recommended is to go back to that original source of motivation and get fired up again.

For most people the return trip to the source is slightly less effective with each repeated exposure. Reading an inspirational book the second time generates less excitement. That audio program is a little less eye opening. We become the self-help versions of opium addicts, constantly "chasing the dragon."

Some will suggest returning our focus to our goal. For the 80%, this can actually become discouraging. Due to the setback we have suffered, our goal can actually be further away than it was. We experience an increased delay in our already overtaxed effort at delayed gratification. Our doubts are given ammunition.

Either of these options assumes that we can marshal the discipline to try and pump ourselves back up. What happens on the day you are just not motivated to motivate yourself? We all know someone (or have been the person) who just doesn't feel good enough to try and make ourselves feel better. How do we motivate ourselves when we don't have the motivation to motivate ourselves?

Here is the bottom line of motivation: You can't rely on it. It tends to abandon you when you need it most. In the quest for consistency, feeling motivated is a plus. It is not a requirement. Imagine this. Someone is going to hitchhike across the country. But they insist they will only accept rides from people driving Bentleys. Now we can all agree that riding in Bentleys would be a great way to travel. The problem is they just don't come along all the time. Motivation is a Bentley. And you can starve waiting for the next one to arrive.

You need a much more reliable source of propulsion if you are going to become consistent. *You need momentum.*

- Motivation is a feeling.

- Momentum is a force that generates its own motivation.

Momentum is a freight train. Do you know how hard it is to stop a freight train? There is a pressurized air hose that runs the length of an entire train. That line is connected to individual brakes on every single wheel of every car of the train. The pressure in that air hose is what keeps the brakes from being applied. In case of an emergency, the engineer performs "a big hole." This is the act of dumping all the air pressure and instantly applying every single brake. How long does it take the train to stop? It depends on the speed of the train, the number of cars, and weight of the cargo, but the short answer is: **miles.**

When you are driven by momentum, what does it take to stop you? Short answer: *A ton.* In fact, like a train, it is much easier to keep going than it is to stop. For the 80%, quitting is easy. For an 80%-er with enough momentum, it is nearly impossible.

George—*I was the original guinea pig for this "Consistency Chain" experiment. As with most projects, I dove into it at a point when I was most energized and excited. The most motivated. But, about 30 days into the project, motivation was less and less of a factor. In fact, motivation was nowhere to be found. Fortunately for me, I was starting to experience the beginnings of momentum.*

Then came Day 361—toughest day by far. I had several back-to-back extended travel days. Travel stress + airplane food + airplane air + the petri dish of fellow travelers = illness. I woke up Day 361 and didn't want to get out of bed. My head hurt. I was nauseous. My body ached. Usually, my workout is the first real activity of the day. Here is the exact transcript and timeline of the conversation that took place in my head:

7am

<u>Momentum</u>: *It's time to work out!*

<u>Me</u>: *I don't know how you got into my house, but I'm calling the police.*

11am

<u>Momentum</u>: *It's time to work out!*

<u>Me</u>: *Shut up and fix me some soup.*

2:30 pm

<u>Momentum</u>: *It's time to work out!*

<u>Me</u>: *Can't you see that I'm watching "Pardon the Interruption"?!*

4pm

<u>Momentum</u>: *It's time to work out!*

<u>Me</u>: *What don't you get?! I'm sick! I'm not working out!*

6pm

Momentum: It's time to work out!

Me: Leave me alone!

6:01 pm

Momentum: Really? Day 361? Four days from a complete year? This is the day you're going to quit? Get out of bed—you can feel terrible on the NordicTrack.

Me: I hate you.

Momentum: I know.

And at 6:02, guess where I was? That's right. The NordicTrack. You could have searched a tri-state area and not found the faintest hint of motivation. It did not have any part to play in my working out that day. Nor did it propel me on the vast majority of the other workouts. I don't need motivation. I need consistency that becomes momentum.

Given the marked advantage of momentum, why have we been so hung-up on motivation? In the beginning, motivation is easier to attain. You read something, you hear something, and poof: You feel something. It is a very simple cause/effect transaction that is immediate and understandable.

The cause/effect of momentum is just as logical. Unfortunately, the payoff is far from immediate. It requires time and unbroken action. It requires consistency. For that reason, very few 80%-ers ever get to fully ride its wave.

Momentum is nothing but the accumulated mass of consistent, focused, purposeful action.

How long does it take to develop momentum? That's easy. Nobody knows. It depends a great deal on the person and the project. That said, here's a truth you can trust: However long it takes to develop momentum—it is soooooo worth it.

Momentum is like having a cadre of personal bodyguards for your mind. Distracting thoughts, discouraging events, and human weakness can all still vie for your attention, but they no longer get to sit down and advise you. Your momentum bodyguard pushes them gently out of your way. All they get is a chance to wave at you as you go by.

If we really loved people, when they sneeze, we wouldn't say, "Gesundheit." We would say, "May momentum be with you." Leaders would be much better served to stop asking the question, "How can I motivate my people?" and focus on this, "How can I assist my people in generating momentum?"

Jim—As an entrepreneur, I loved it when momentum was driving my businesses. There's no better feeling than when all cylinders are firing. The key is getting to that point. How do you get people to stay motivated until momentum takes over?

That question was one I started to explore years ago when I first started participating in sales contests. For some reason, I had a personal obsession with sales contests. I loved them and always believed I could win the prize and recognition that came with it. But I was amazed how others quickly lost interest. It was like some of them gave up even before the contest started. I just chalked it up to people not being disciplined enough. Little did I know that people were just wired differently. It was only when I was trying to get healthier and admitted my traditional methods of reaching a goal didn't work for me, did I come to realize that just perhaps there was another way to gain momentum.

Chapter 10

Einstein

Who is the smartest man of the last century? Most people would name Albert Einstein.

George—Not to brag, but when I was younger, a lot of teachers said I reminded them of Einstein. I asked, "How so?" They said because he didn't do well in school either.

This is an important teaching point. When someone pays you a compliment, don't ask a lot of questions.

When we think of Einstein, we think of this towering intellect, this amazing brain. In fact, we insult people by saying, "You're no Einstein." But the fact is, at one point, even Einstein wasn't Einstein. At age 26, he was marking his days as a low-paid patent clerk. He had to develop, change and refine his brain before he became Einstein.

Our brain is not static and fixed. The brain itself is composed of many different components, each with different attributes and responsibilities. Joining and making all these elements work together is a neural network of billions of connections. And unlike train tracks that were laid down decades ago and rarely change, these connections are adjusting and morphing daily. We rewire our brain constantly. We shape and refine our brain over the course of a lifetime. Unfortunately, for most this is not a conscious, considered process.

One of the most dramatic demonstrations of creating new connections is the brain in the aftermath of a stroke. Victims can lose most of the control of the left side of their body, including speech function. Now obviously, the body is still intact. The limbs, muscles, tendons and nerves are still there. What is lost is the connection within the brain. Stroke rehabilitation is the process of creating new connections, rerouting neural pathways. With rehabilitation, amazing progress can be made. In some cases, the patient's motor control is indistinguishable from their ability pre-stroke.

Scientists call the brain's ability to change "neuroplasticity." It is the seat of habit formation. A habit is a neural pathway that has been formed and strengthened by repetition. An idea or impulse is formed, followed by the action. Done over and over, this pattern of action bypasses the level of conscious thought or evaluation. It simply results in the programed behavior. With repetition, we create a cause/effect sequence that becomes so ingrained, it is extremely difficult to interrupt.

Addiction is the extreme version of this process. An inciting idea or impulse is called a "trigger." Then, through a cascade of failures, beginning in the hedonic center and ending in the higher reasoning part of our brain, or the pre-frontal cortex, the self-destructive act recurs.

For anyone who has ever tried to understand the behavior of an addict, it can feel infuriating. You want to ask, "What the hell were you thinking?!" The reality is they weren't "thinking" at all. Not in the context of evaluating risk, assessing value, and considering the consequences to themselves or others.

How different is that process in us? Don't we at times find ourselves acting in ways that don't support what we really want? Whether it is avoiding the phone call we should make, eating the donut, wasting hours on Facebook, or simple procrastination, it is very easy to be "triggered" into an unhelpful behavior or activity.

Now the good news...First, we have access to the machinery that creates our undermining behaviors. And second, we have the power to rewire and then reverse this process.

Here's an image to help visualize this task. Picture a single thread. That is the neuron chain the very first time you perform the act that you want to ingrain. The next day, you repeat the action and now the neuron chain is two threads. After a week, it is a thin cord. After a month, a cable. After a year, a solid, sturdy chain. Brain researchers have a phrase, "neurons that fire together, wire together."

How long does it take to build a robust chain? Some motivational speakers say that it takes 21 days. Others say it's 30 days. The real answer is that it depends on the person and the degree of effort required.

Randy Pennington, an expert on change and organizational performance, puts it this way: If you're told that eating dark chocolate is healthy for you, how long would it take to develop that habit, build that neural pathway? For most of us, about a day. But if we were told that 45 minutes a day of vigorous exercise is important to our health, how long would it take to build that neural pathway? That ingrained habit could easily take six months to a year. Or more.

When pondering the question of how long it will take, here's a better question: Does it matter? If we are addressing a vital part of our life with a very achievable approach that is going to yield lifelong benefits, does it matter? If it takes you five years to build your dream business instead of three, is it any less sweet?

George—In my "ER" quest of becoming healthier, fitter, stronger, the fitness habit certainly didn't take hold in 21 or 30 days. There was a tipping point at about four months. That is when I remember asking myself a different question each day. Early on, the question was, "Will I work out today?" This is a very dangerous question because it has a 50% possibility of failure. Then one day my question had changed. It was now, "What workout am I going to do today?" This is a great question because it has a 100% success rate.

In weight training, mentally focusing on the muscle being worked actually increases the effectiveness of the exercise. In the same way, when you are trying to develop a new consistent action, hold that image of a thread becoming stronger and stronger.

For the 80%, the default setting in our brain has been toward inconsistency. We can absolutely change that. Up to this point, our brain has been the opposition.

Now, we make it our ally.

Chapter 11
Skepticism

If you are in the 80% who have actively sought out a success system that would work for you, then you've had your heart broken. More than a few times. Each attempt follows the same downward trajectory:

- Excitement and hope > Resistance
- Resistance >Inconsistent effort
- Inconsistent effort >Discouragement
- Discouragement >Failure

Do these success systems work? Yes, they totally work. Just not for the 80%. Each system assumes that it will actually be applied in a consistent manner. Check, please!

As the failures amass, it's easy to become skeptical or cynical or both. At first, we blame the system. Then, if we have a degree of self-awareness, we will finally realize there is only one common denominator in all these train wrecks. Us. That is when we move from skepticism (I don't think this will work) to cynicism (Nothing works).

George—*I've been told that I'm skeptical, but I doubt it.*

It's okay to be skeptical. In fact, we have a more positive name for this: It's called being "discerning."

Discernment is a mature, experienced evaluation of opportunity and risk. It is a powerful skill we should all develop. The danger lies in cynicism. This is the blanket rejection of something new and different. If this is our gatekeeper, then nothing is allowed to come in. While it might save us from some useless ideas, it will also block real opportunities.

As you evaluate the Consistency Chain prescription for 80% inconsistency, use discernment.

- What is the up-side potential?
- What is the downside risk?
- What is the cost?
- What is the timeframe?

If you evaluate in those terms, you will take action. Even if you don't really believe it's going to work.

George—*I have an entire walk-in closet full of failed systems. Name it, and I've done it.*

- *Vision board—Check.*
- *Motivational tapes, CDs, MP3s—Technology moved on. Me, not so much.*
- *Subliminal messaging—I never could hear what they were trying to tell me.*
- *Career Coach—After six months, I caused him to quit the business.*
- *Self-help books—"Seven Ways to Fill Up A Shelf With Stuff You'll Never Read!"*
- *Seminars—At the break, do you think they'll have cookies?*
- *Ab Blaster—Don't ask.*

- *Motivational posters—"Teamwork! It's how we spread the blame!"*
- *Goal-setting programs—Where do you want to be in 10 years? Dude, I'm not sure where I am now.*
- *Meditation—Be sure and set an alarm so you know when to wake up.*
- *Affirmations—Everyday, in every way, I can't believe I'm talking to myself.*

And let's not forget time-management systems (Franklin, Daytimer, online, offline, PDA-based, paper-based). I bought all the different colored pens and spent entire weeks assigning ABC priorities, followed by number rankings of urgency, followed by shapes of importance, ending with doodles of boredom.

Here is what a typical planner entry looked like:

   Monday's Tasks:

- *A1 Red—Try and find your planner.*
- *A2 Blue—Seriously, it has to be here somewhere.*
- *A3 Green—Tomorrow we really have to find that planner.*
- *A4 Purple—What's on TV?*

If you could buy it and fail with it, I have one.

The worst part of these repeated failures is that they undermine belief in ourselves. So, if a course of action requires that you <u>have faith</u> that you can do it, you're already in trouble. People sometimes try and encourage the 80%-er with this gem, "You just have to believe!"

And what if you don't? Or more precisely, what if you can't? When faced with a track record of your unsuccessful attempts, it is only human to have doubt.

How do we get past doubt and develop belief? By releasing results and taking consistent action. Releasing results is really just reframing your goal as discussed in the "ER" chapter. We can develop consistent action by leveraging the power of our insatiable desire for instant gratification. Neither of these concepts requires the presence of belief. In fact, you can doubt the entire journey. You'll still arrive.

That is really the hidden power of the Consistency Chain—the 800 Million-Dollar Idea we mentioned in Chapter 4. You don't have to believe it will work. You certainly don't have to believe it will work for you. You just have to be willing to give it three days. That's it. No belief. No long-term commitment. Just three days.

George—*When I began my experiment, I had zero faith that I could do it. Don't get me wrong. I knew someone else could. Just not me. I was pretty sure I would fail. It is a miracle that I finally decided, "What the heck. I've failed at a ton of things like this, what's one more? Give it a shot."*

Jim—*When I started my new Chain, I was excited to try it because I had George as a role model. If he can do it, I can, too. I also was going to give it a go because nothing else had worked for me. So I did. Along the way, I have been tempted to integrate more things. "Perhaps I should drop down and do some sit ups! If I did that, I could enter 'SU' on my calendar and write it in green ink. Maybe I should get a Fitbit and track steps! Then I could calculate the mean average of my daily output and set a sub-goal to exceed by an ever-increasing percentage!" In short, I've been tempted to screw this thing up. But I stuck it out for three days. And here I am, still staying the course. And it's working.*

If your belief in yourself is low, not a problem. If your track record is littered with disappointments, perfect! Tell your inner cynic to take a three-day vacation.

George—*My best friend in high school was interested in photography and wanted to build a darkroom in his parents' house. He asked and was told no. Then his parents went away for a three-day weekend. When they returned, their laundry room was several feet shorter than it used to be. And there was a new door. In three days, he had framed in, drywalled, taped, painted and plumbed a new darkroom. His folks were mad. But, faced with this fait accompli, there was little they could do. They got over their anger, and he got his darkroom.*

Two lessons:

1. Sometimes it really is better to ask for forgiveness rather than permission.

2. Never underestimate what you can do in three days.

Chapter 12

Pick a Lane

Have you ever heard some idiot say, "Man, I really have to get my life together?"

George– _Man, I say that all the time!_

Shocker.

What does that phrase even mean? Get our lives "together"? We are already the total sum of all of our actions, choices and experiences, all wrapped into one person. How much more "together" could we be? More likely, the phrase we are looking for is, "I would like to have more power and control over parts of my life I'm not satisfied with." Other than the pure 20%-ers, most of us can identify with that statement.

Assuming there is a way to gain this control (spoiler alert: there is), then what are the main areas of our lives that demand attention? The good news is that the number is relatively small.

Here's one list:

- Physical Wellness & Health
- Relationships
- Career
- Finances

- Spirituality
- Mental Wellbeing

Your list may differ slightly. And that's okay—it's your list. For most people, however, that about covers it. Six items or areas tops. Suddenly we have reduced "getting my life together" from overwhelming down to merely "whelming." Given the fact that most of us already have an area of our life where we operate with 20% consistency, this list becomes even more manageable.

Just for fun, let's take each area and brainstorm some Chain Activities that might have a significant impact in that part of your life.

Physical Wellness & Health:

Direction: I want to be healthier.

Possible activities:

- Workout every day.
- Make informed, conscious decisions to eat healthier.
- Walk for 30 minutes three times a week.

Relationships:

Direction: I want my relationships to be stronger and more meaningful.

Possible activities:

- Spend 15 minutes of distraction-free time listening and talking with my spouse/significant other.
- Spend 15 "non-screen minutes" playing, listening and interacting with my child.
- Once a day, reach out to a friend.

Jim– *One of the best things I ever did was to pick one day each week and take my son Jeff out to breakfast and then on to school. The following week, I took my other son, Adam. This was amazing one-on-one time. It was an opportunity for conversations to occur that would never happen in another setting.*

For a hard-charging 20%-er, this could easily have been perceived as just another activity jammed into an already over-stuffed schedule. In fact, it was a tremendous gift—for <u>me</u>. *As important as it was for my boys, I received as much, if not more, benefit.*

It cost almost no money (they always picked McDonalds) and very little time. And my boys and I are still reaping the benefits. As investments go, this one is tough to beat.

After week two, Sherry said, "When is my turn?" It's important to have balance in your life. As my wife, Sherry has been giving me 47 years of checks and balances. And no, she never picked McDonalds.

<u>Career</u>:

Direction: I want to build a lucrative, thriving network marketing business.

Possible activities:

- Reach out to two new prospects daily.
- Add one person to my prospect list.
- Personally contact a person in my downline.

<u>Financial</u>:

Direction: I want higher savings and more security.

Possible activities:

- Spend 30 minutes a day learning about investments.

- Develop and monitor a budget.
- Keep a spending and expense diary.

Spirituality:

Direction: I want a more meaningful spiritual life.

Possible activities:

- Read faith-based books 30 minutes a day.
- Spend time in prayer or meditation.
- Keep a gratitude journal.

Mental Wellbeing:

Direction: I want my brain to be sharper and constantly learning.

Possible activities:

- Spend 30 minutes reading challenging books.
- Learn a new language.
- Make daily entries in a life journal.

The bottom line is for every area of our life, there is some specific, doable activity that would have significant impact. And we KNOW this. Up to now, we just haven't acted on it.

Worst case scenario, say you are as big an 80%-er as George...

George—*Hey, I resent that.*

...And it takes you a solid year to make progress in one area of your life. Then, with that practice firmly imbedded, you move on to another area of your life. So, it could take you five or six years to make balanced improvement in all aspects of your existence.

So what?! Who cares how long it would take to achieve something that 99% of world never attain. And secondly, it doesn't take five or six years. It takes one day. Today.

- Today, my business is dynamic and growing.
- Today, I am stronger, fitter and healthier.
- Today, my relationships are stronger and richer.
- Today, I am wealthier in both money and knowledge.
- Today, I am deeper and stronger in my faith.
- Today, I am smarter, and my skills are more powerful.

We must force ourselves to pull our eyes away from that daunting five- or six-year goal and focus on the action we will take today. At the risk of sounding like a motivational speaker, when we do what's possible today, the implausible future suddenly becomes inevitable.

The choice is yours as to what aspect of your life you would like to first address. But you know. The fact that you bought a book focused on network marketing is a <u>very</u> strong indicator.

Furthermore, if you have any question, here is an approach for deciding what you tackle first:

1) Am I sitting on a gold mine?

Is there an opportunity I have right now that is not producing because I am not engaged in it consistently?

2) Is there an area in my life that is heading for trouble?

Do I have an important relationship that is not healthy? Am I near disaster in my health, career or finances?

For the more intuitive, here is a great technique. When you are torn between two possible courses of action, flip a coin. Before you uncover the coin, ask yourself, "What do I hope it is?" When you look at the coin, are you relieved or disappointed? There is your answer. The bottom line is, you know. There is a pull in that direction.

Once you have set the compass for where you want to go, the next step is to decide on the 20% activity to which you will commit.

George—*Don't let the word "commit" trip you up. For years, it was a stumbling block for me. I would look at something and say, "Yeah, I might like to do that, but I don't know that I'd want to do it forever." In the context of the Consistency Chain, "forever commitment" is not required. We're not even demanding "tomorrow commitment" from ourselves. Just today. I just have to decide on a high-leverage, 20% activity that I am capable and willing to do today. Just today.*

Jim—*Ray Kroc said the secret to success is being at the right place at the right time and doing something about it. This is the right place. This is the right time. All we have to do is make the "right" decision and follow through with immediate action.*

Who knows? A day at a time, maybe you'll wake up five or six years from now a healthier, wealthier, smarter, successful, centered, happy person—who speaks fluent Italian.

George—*Buongiorno!*

Chapter 13
Seinfeld and 'The $800 Million Idea'

G<u>eorge</u>—*Everyone has deep, embarrassing secrets that they would prefer to keep hidden. Here is mine: For 10 years I did stand-up comedy. This was actually one of the most fun, most exciting times of my life. That was back in the day when every city had a comedy club. Or two. Or three. It seemed like everyone willing to go on stage at open mic night was offered a sitcom.*

Except me.

I am a firm believer that everything we do, every experience we have, every skill we build, prepares us for the next phase of our lives. Stand-up certainly did that for me.

About six years into that 10-year career, I had a life-altering experience. At the time, the Atlanta Punchline had two comedy clubs. They put all the comics in one shop-worn house. Picture an unsupervised college dorm without all the annoying classes. It would be filled with a constant rotation of six performers. On Mondays, the club was usually dark. But this particular week that I was there, they were hosting a special event: One night. One show. Jerry Seinfeld.

Five other nomadic comics and I made the walk down the hill to the club. We climbed the back stairs up to a private balcony. We sat down, crossed our arms and assumed a position of, "Okay, Comedy God, show us something."

Seinfeld performed about an hour and 20 minutes. The show was over. All six of us climbed down the stairs and trudged back up the hill. As we walked, the most remarkable thing occurred. For two blocks, nobody said anything. Total silence. That is not the normal behavior of always-talkative comics.

The spell broke when, finally, one guy put words to what we were all thinking. "Guys, we are so screwed." We had just witnessed a person who had totally mastered an art that the rest of us wrestled with on a nightly basis.

I admit to many flaws. But lack of self-awareness isn't one of them. On that long walk back up to the house, I knew two things.

1) *The gap between my skills and Seinfeld's skills was immense.*

2) *I had absolutely no idea how to bridge that gap.*

I did stand-up for four more years. But that night was the beginning of me exploring other career options.

Another three decades would pass before I read the Seinfeld interview that answered the question, "How do I bridge that gap" and inspired this book.

In an interview, Jerry Seinfeld recounts a question he received from a new comedian. The young comic asked, "How do I get to be you?" Seinfeld responded, "First of all, that's not the goal." Getting to be "Jerry Seinfeld" wasn't even Jerry Seinfeld's goal. It was never about the sitcom or the cars or the charter jets.

Jerry told the kid, "I had one goal. Be a better comic. And I looked at all the things I could do to accomplish that, and I settled on one thing: Write jokes every day. I bought a calendar. The first day that

I wrote jokes, I put an "X" on the calendar. The second day that I wrote, I put an "X" on the calendar."

And here is where the spark of genius emerges. Most people would look at that calendar and see two "X"s. Jerry did not. He saw a chain of two links. From that point forward, he had one very simple, very specific goal:

Don't Break the Chain.

And now, you get to find out why we refer to this as "The $800 Million Idea." It's for a very simple reason. When Seinfeld sold the syndication rights for his sitcom, he received $800 million. As a reward for consistent effort, that is certainly a nice one. That doesn't include all the money he earned traveling the country as a stand-up comic or all the paychecks he received during the actual nine-year run of the show. So, really, calling this "The $800 Million Idea" is underestimating its worth.

We wish we could charge you $800 million for this concept for two reasons.

1) People tend to attach value to the things they pay dearly for.

2) We would have $800 million (which could cut George's credit card debt almost in half).

Don't let the simplicity of this concept fool you. It is the 80% solution. In the context of what we've already covered, let's examine his plan.

- Seinfeld did not set a SMART goal or a BHAG. He set an "ER" goal. He didn't put up pictures of Porsches and massive estates on Long Island. He set a direction. "I want to be a bettER comedian."

- He didn't have a massive, complicated tracking system. He had a calendar and a pen. He kept it simple.

- When faced with adversity and inevitable setbacks, he focused on his Chain activity. He wrote jokes. He made it to breakfast every day.

- Of all the possible actions he could have taken, he focused on a 20% high-leverage task. Writing jokes was going to result in massive results.

In a very competitive business, his relentless effort separated him from all his rivals. His momentum pushed him through the comedy ranks and finally onto TV. The compound interest on his efforts could not be ignored.

George—*I read the interview with Seinfeld and have a confession to make—I almost missed it. I almost let it go by without even giving his approach a try. It seemed too simple. "Sure, it worked for Seinfeld, but he's one of the best comedians in history." And that is a mistake many people make. We look at where someone is now, and assume they were always like that.*

Then I remembered a documentary I had watched. After the sitcom wrapped up, Jerry performed one final show using all his tried and trusted material. Then he did something virtually no comic has ever dared. He threw all that time-tested material in the trash. He started over, from the blank page. It is fascinating to watch as he battled his way through the development of a new show. He stumbled. He hesitated. Audiences couldn't understand how someone so good could be so bad. In a word, he bombed. It was painful to watch. Having gone through the exact same progression, I can assure you that it was painful for Jerry to experience.

That's when I realized the process for both of us was exactly the same. Nothing is given. As a comic, you have to be bad before you get good. You have to write and work and polish before you see any real results. As bad as the experience was, I'm guessing Jerry never got discouraged. He had done this before. He knew he would eventually get everything right. As long as he didn't break the Chain.

And I finally had the answer to the question I had asked years before, "Why was there such an immense gap in results between Seinfeld and myself?" Consistency. The distance between his accomplishments and mine was the compound interest of years and years of consistency.

For those embarking on the network marketing journey, it is tempting to over-edify the leaders on stage. They have accomplished a great deal. They deserve your respect. They are so natural and make it look so easy. They are where you aspire to be.

But, remember, you are viewing the finished product. It wasn't always that way.

Jim—*I don't believe anyone is an overnight success. We see people on stage collecting their accolades but we're not seeing the entire picture. We don't see the process, the habits, and the work that led to that event. We all want the results. But results are built on daily actions.*

The award winners in life had the same challenges, the same fears, and the same obstacles that we face. They just overcame them by unrelenting consistency. The gap may be large. But it is bridgeable.

Don't break the Chain.

Chapter 14

Give Us Three Days

For years we've been asking the impossible of the 80%. We demand that they decide on a distant goal and commit to daily effort. We ask them to do this for months, for years, if not forever. For the 80%, it is difficult to imagine a formula less likely to succeed. Is it any wonder the results have been dismal?

Forget daily effort for years. Or months. In fact, don't even worry about the rest of the week. The only thing to concern yourself with is the next three days. Just three. Even the most doubtful, inconsistent, commitment-phobic 80%-er has to believe themselves capable of this.

The Three Days

Day One: Decide and Act

The day to do this, by the way, is today. Not tomorrow. Not next week. Today. Unless it is 11:59pm, this today. NOW!

There is a reality TV show that follows homicide detectives trying to solve a murder. It's called The First 48. Every episode begins with this statement, "If the detectives don't find a lead in the first 48 hours, the chance of solving the crime drops by 50%."

If you are an 80%-er and you don't begin TODAY, the chances of you ever doing this drop by 80%!

George—*Disclaimer: The authors admit they have conducted absolutely no scientific research to support the preceding statement. But, from personal experience, it feels about right. In fact, it may be a little low.*

Jim—*There's an old network market saying that more people quit in the first 48 hours than any other time. That's just another way of saying, "They stop before they start."*

We've all heard the phrase "Ready, willing and able." Here's some good news, you don't have to be ready or able. You just have to be willing. You don't have to believe that this is going to work. You just have to start.

So, what do you do on Day One?

1) List the areas of your life that matter most to you (health, relationships, financial, etc.).

2) Decide on the area of your life over which you want to gain control and mastery (given the fact that you are reading a book that has *"for Network Marketing"* in the title, this should be a no-brainer step.)

3) Define that direction (network marketing as an example) using "ER" or "more" words.

- Be a bettER recruiter.

- Be a MORE skilled communicator.

- Be a bettER and MORE empathetic listener.

4) Consider the possible Chain activities that would support that direction and choose one that is a high leverage/high impact 20% activity. You don't ever want to be in the position of "doing the wrong thing well."

5) Start NOW. Put down this book and do it.

__George__—Seriously, just start! It's not about perfection. It's about propulsion. Sometimes, we 80%-ers feel like we have to "put our ducks" in a row. Just be aware that duck-herding is a very low paying career.

It is much better to start, stumble and adjust than it is to delay. If a car is sitting still, what does it take to turn it around? You're probably going to need about 20 strong people to lift and rotate it. But if it is rolling, you can fine-tune the direction with one finger on the wheel. The journey is going to give you feedback to refine your actions. But not if you don't take these first steps.

Just start. Start TODAY. Do your Consistency Chain action. Then put your "X" on the calendar. Click the button on your Consistency Chain App. Then pat yourself on the back. You've taken the first step toward changing your life.

Day Two: Build the Chain

Your direction and "ER" goal are established. On Day Two, you repeat your Chain activity. Then you put your second "X" on the calendar or enter a second mark on your app. What do you have? A Chain. You did it! You have nailed the most important steps required for you to gain control of your life and your previously inconsistent existence. A little applause is called for!

Day Three: Don't Break the Chain

It doesn't get much simpler than this. <u>Don't break the Chain!</u> You took action the first day. You confirmed that you are capable of consistency by repeating the action on Day Two. There should be zero doubt about what you can do on Day Three. Remember, we're not talking about the rest of your life. Just one day. Today. Day Three.

On Day Three, we can do something amazing. We can forget about the intimidating direction we have chosen. By keeping our thoughts focused on the daily activity, the direction will take care of itself. That's the paradox. Because we aren't obsessed with the goal, we are much more likely to attain it.

To be clear, just like there is no tomorrow, there is no Day Four. It doesn't exist. Remember the movie, "Groundhog Day"? Bill Murray's character woke up to the same day, every single day. For him, every day was Groundhog Day. As fans of the movie may remember, he went through several phases of dealing with this new reality. First, he was confused by it. Then he resisted it. Then he embraced it.

He finally came to understand that his life was lived in just one day. He could destroy it. He could waste it. Or, he could live it to the fullest. He had one day and only one day. When he finally accepted that fact, his life was transformed. He became the person he was meant to be. When we wake up tomorrow, it won't be Groundhog Day. But it will be Day Three.

If you can win Day Three, you can win your life. This is the only day that counts. From now on, we just win Day Three. There is no regretting the past. There is no worrying about the future. There is no pressure. We are simply going to keep winning Day Three until that magical thing called *momentum* shows up. You don't know when it will arrive. You don't even have to believe it will arrive. But it is on the way. And when it knocks on the door, your life will change forever.

Win Day Three.

Don't break the Chain.

Chapter 15
The Chain Defined

The Consistency Chain is simple. The following five tips are not meant to complicate; they are meant to clarify. They are here to assist you in maximizing the Chain.

1. Choose a Meaningful Direction

Make sure that you focus on something that really matters to you. That way, when you succeed, the payoff will have meaningful benefit. While the Chain concept is simple, it's not always easy. On those challenging days, it helps to have a direction that resonates with you. Make this first Chain, this first win, really count. This won't be the only Chain you will ever undertake. Realizing great results in this first Chain will energize and power you in the establishment of subsequent Chains.

2. Keep It Simple

Remember what we are doing. We are literally rewiring our brains. We are building and strengthening new neural pathways. Your Consistency Chain action has to be very well defined and specific. You can't rewire your brain if your Chain activity has 27 moving parts, three options and four alternate variations. You are trying to develop a stimulus>response sequence. If you think "workout," the response needs to be "go to the gym."

- Stimulus thought: Workout

  Immediate action: Head to the gym

- Stimulus thought: Invite

  Immediate action: Call, text or message someone

- Stimulus thought: Engage

  Immediate action: Really be present with your spouse or child

- Stimulus thought: Read

  Immediate action: Pick up the dang book

George—Jim and I were both a part of a network marketing company. They came out with a daily planner/activity tracker called, "The Daily 8." It was a beautiful product. I bought two. I couldn't wait to get home and put this amazing new tool to work. Then my 80% nature kicked in. Eight things? Every day? I knew that there was zero chance I would ever be able to do that. So, I did what every true 80%-er would do. Nothing. In fact, I was so discouraged with what I knew that I couldn't do, I didn't do the things I could do. There is a classic sales adage that says, "The confused mind says 'no'." Our corollary is, "The overwhelmed 80% mind says don't go."

If you're interested, I still have both planners—in perfect condition, never written in.

Early on, I was trying to explain my 80% brain to Jim. As an example, I told him, "For the 80%, the only thing wrong with 'The Daily 8' planner was that it is seven too many."

Jim—You know who designed that planner, right?

George— Oops. Sorry.

3. Define the Activity

There should not be any "wiggle room" in your brain about whether you really completed your activity on any given day. If there is, the 80% mind will find the "small print" and undermine your efforts.

Just like there is no point cheating in Solitaire, there is no value in putting together a Chain that you secretly know is not real.

There are usually two ways to define completion of the action: time-defined and activity-defined.

1) **Time-Defined:** This has become known as the "Pomodoro Technique."

George—The name comes from the Italian word for tomato. The man that coined the phrase used a kitchen timer shaped like a tomato. This was years ago. If he were naming it for his timer today, it would probably be called the "Apple Watcho" technique.

We simply commit to a defined amount of uninterrupted time that we are going to spend on a specific task. The standard unit is 25 minutes. This means that you can complete two 25-minute time cycles, or pomodoros, in an hour, with a five-minute break to refresh. (For example: 25-min. of taskwork + 5-min. break + 25-min. of taskwork + 5-min break = 60 minutes.) This is ideal for "desk-bound" tasks. Other activities lend themselves better to longer time frames.

Example:

- I will work out for 45 minutes in an activity that raises my heart rate and causes me to sweat.

- I will read for 30 minutes in a book that increases my skills in an area that directly affects my career or business.

This approach is perfect for activities that have no "finish line" or for projects that are too big to finish in one burst of action. For example, this book was written in a series of pomodoros over several weeks.

2) **Activity-Defined:** Perfect for actions that have very well-defined stop points.

Marketing Example:

- I will invite two people to look at my opportunity.

- I will add one person to my prospect list.

For both these methods, the key concern is to be honest with yourself: You either did the action or you didn't.

Your accountability must be very black and white. Ever heard of the 11th Commandment of Success: *Thou shalt not kid thyself?* Perhaps not—but now you have. If you start shading the truth, you are undermining yourself. It would be better to have a Chain with a couple of breaks, than a perfect Chain that you know is a lie.

4. Start Small

In the beginning, it is better to set an activity action that is well within your capacity. The activity itself should not seriously "stretch" you. The "stretching" is in performing the action consistently. There is more than enough doubt and disbelief in the beginning of this process. There is no need to intensify it by selecting a daily activity that is at the limits of your ability.

The power of the Chain is not in any single day's action. The power is in the consistency of the action, day after day. Can you invite one person to look at your business? Of course you can. You know you can do that. This is not an activity that requires belief. It is rooted in knowledge. And, if you win every Day 3, over the course of a year, you would have invited 365 people to join you. Can you imagine what your business is going to look like then? Words like "awesome", "amazing," and "scary good" come to mind.

In network marketing, there are many leaders who encourage massive action. The challenge with that is that it is unsustainable. And for the 80% people in your group, it is not duplicatable. There may be people who are capable of contacting 100 people a day. But, which would you prefer to have, the person who approaches 100 people a day or 100 people who approach one person a day?

George—*My answer is easy. I would always take the 100 people taking a small action on a consistent basis. Why? Because that is something that is duplicatable. Network marketing is a different kind of business. The golden rule is "It's not what works, it's what duplicates." As an 80%-er, I know I can't talk to 100 people a day. So, if that is what is required to be successful, I'm not interested.*

But how would I react if you tell me that the key to your success is that you talk to one person a day. In addition, you tell me that you will teach me how to do exactly the same thing. Now I'm interested. I know I could do that. That "small" activity is totally realistic and can be duplicated.

Jim—*This won't be accepted by a lot of leaders, but I don't like the philosophy of taking massive action for 90 days or whatever. I don't even like the thought of listing 100 names on a sheet of paper. Network marketing is almost always "in addition to" whatever a person is currently doing. If we ask for too much, we usually end up with nothing.*

5. Track Your Progress

There are a couple of options here. Or maybe best of all, use both of them.

    1) Calendar

A simple wall calendar is perfect. We recommend printing a month at a time. Then simply mark an "X" on the calendar every day you succeed in performing your Chain activity. Watching that unbroken Chain get longer and longer is an unbelievable confidence builder.

George—*The calendars from my first Chain are still up on the wall in my office. I'm not sure there is anything that causes me to feel more pride. And when I'm feeling down or discouraged, just looking at that wall is a huge shot of confidence. "If I did that, I can certainly accomplish the task at hand!"*

2) The Consistency Chain App

This is a free tool that is available for both Apple and Android products. Simply go to our website, (ConsistencyChain.com) click on the link, and download the correct version for your phone. This is perfect to record your daily victory immediately. And the monthly view will allow you to bask in your ever-lengthening Chain.

Or both! You cannot celebrate changing the direction of your life too often!

(One thing to know about the app, once you download it, you have 24 hours to perform your first Chain activity. If you don't, the app goes away. Poof! We're serious, start NOW!)

Chapter 16

One Chain at a Time

The temptation will be to tackle additional Chains, too soon. As you experience success, the temptation will be thinking, "This is working! What else can I add?!"

Don't.

If you have just one Chain to which you are committed, the odds of your succeeding are very high. There may be a rare occasional stumble, but you will experience a degree of consistency that you have never experienced before.

George—I built an amazing first Chain. After six months of perfect performance, I decided it was time to add a second Chain. For me, that was too soon. The second Chain was nothing but stops and starts. In a word, inconsistent.

My advice for 80%-ers would be to give the first Chain six months, if not a solid year. That is long enough for most actions to be habituated. How do you know you've reached that point? Stop tracking it on the calendar. If you are still performing the action on a daily basis, you have a habit. For me, I no longer have to plan to work out. Instead, I am someone who works out. No thought, no decision, no problem, just consistent action.

No surprise, 20%-ers are going to be very tempted to try and build multiple Chains at the same time. They are probably capable of keeping all those balls in the air.

Jim—*For me, one year seems way too long to wait before adding more Chains. As a 20%-er, it's hard to believe that I can't handle more than one area in my life at a time. But part of that thinking is based on the fact that some areas I "handle" naturally, without any real conscious decision.*

With my health goals, I want to go faster. I think I can handle more. After all, I've proven I can handle numerous business-building tasks all at the same time. Why shouldn't I be able to handle a number of health-related tasks at one time? But then I say to myself, "Jim, you have had the same weight loss goal for years. You've tried to tackle it with the same strategies that have brought you success in business. How has that worked for you?"

What I've come to understand is what works for the 20% people doesn't necessarily work for the 80% people. And what works in the 20% areas of my life doesn't necessarily work in the 80% areas of my life.

To be honest, I love having only one health related activity to perform each day. I feel such a sense of accomplishment taking a step forward each day. I do think about adding more tasks other than just walking, but I'm holding steady. And compared to my previous efforts, my consistency is off the charts. Besides, a year goes by pretty fast.

Don't tell George, but I am applying the Consistency Chain to areas of my life other than health. These are areas in which I am more naturally diligent. It can be done and it's fun.

George—*Did I mention that Jim is a 20%-er?*

For perspective, consider this: What if it does take an entire year to build a bulletproof network marketing Chain? Is that too high a time investment to gain control over an important part of your life and build the foundation of your financial future? Worst case, it might take a total of five or six years to really attain mastery of your total life. At that point, you would have gained what most people will never achieve in an entire lifetime.

Revisiting Navy SEAL wisdom, these elite have a saying, "Slow is smooth. Smooth is fast." Over the long haul, the marathoner beats the sprinter. The tortoise beats the hare. One perfect Chain beats the crap out of two or three incomplete efforts.

Participation 24/7

The fastest, most certain path to consistency is to take action every day. EVERY DAY. Not every other day. Not most days. Not six days a week. Every day. The good news is, for network marketers, this is a non-issue. Virtually every possible Chain activity lends itself to 24/7 participation.

But what if you select a Chain activity that doesn't lend itself to seven-day-a-week performance? In that unlikely case, we recommend, "support links." These are substitute actions that support your Chain activity.

George—Here is my story about support links and momentum. After working out every single day for over a year, I decided I needed a slight adjustment. There is such a thing as overtraining. I didn't want to get hurt. I wanted to get stronger, healthier and fitter. With that in mind, I decided that I would take one day a week as a rest day. On that "support link" day I would read and research health and nutrition.

So, my rest day arrived. And guess what I did? I worked out. I planned to take the day off, but I just couldn't. My mind argued,

"Look, you can take a rest day. Just not today. We feel great. Let's work out, and you can take your rest day tomorrow."

It took me three weeks before I could finally bring myself to take my "support link" day. That's when I knew, beyond any doubt, that I had turned myself into a 20%-er in the area of health. When momentum arrives, it's a freight train. And it will arrive for you, too.

Jim—*I'm only a few months into my "walk three miles per day" Chain. From the beginning, I decided this was to be a six-day a week activity. On two occasions, I have actually allowed myself a "rest day." But, even then, I felt the pull to add to the Chain. So, while I didn't complete my entire circuit, I still walked. Already, I was feeling the pull of momentum. I do like knowing that, if I need to, I can take a day off. That releases some of the pressure.*

Release the Results

In the beginning, there may be a temptation to judge your Chain by external metrics. If your direction is to build a network marketing team, the question is: *"How many people did I sponsor this month?"* If your direction is attaining health and fitness, the question is: "How many pounds did I lose?"

There is a time for measurements and assessment. This isn't it. For the first few months, this isn't really about building a business or a healthier body. It's about building a Chain.

There are only two questions you need to concern yourself with:

- Am I performing a daily activity that any reasonable person would agree will inevitably take me in the direction I desire?
- Did I perform my Chain activity today?

If you can answer, "yes" to both, that is all you need to know. Those are the only results that matter.

__Jim__—In the successful areas of my life, I have been very results-oriented. That thinking has not been beneficial in the 80% area of my life related to health and fitness. I am consciously learning to move my focus onto the daily practice and not the results. I am not obsessing with the measurements of a healthier body. I am concentrating solely on my Chain activity. I know that if I do that, the healthier body will arrive.

Ripples

Even though we are "releasing the results," we do want to be on the lookout for "ripples." Let's say you have built a perfect Chain of connecting with one new person a day. After a reasonable period of time, say a couple of months, there should be a "ripple" indicating that the results are on their way. If there doesn't seem to be a hint of movement, this is not a consistency issue, this is probably a technique issue.

Go upline to an active, skilled distributor. Trust us, they are going to be very excited to help a serious, consistently engaged team member. Let them help you refine and hone your approach. The great news is that you are in a much better position to receive coaching at this point. You have already overcome the number one challenge, doing nothing. Now you're ready to take your skills to the next level.

The Early Bird Gets the Chain

Study after study documents that willpower is finite. Each person only has a limited supply. What is used for one activity cannot be used for another.

__Jim__—It is no coincidence that both George and I schedule our Chain activities early in the day. I walk at 6:30 a.m. George works *out and writes first thing in the morning. Not only are we drawing on a full stock of willpower, we can savor the rest of the day. No matter what happens later, we have already won.*

Some activities don't lend themselves to early morning execution. That doesn't mean you can't succeed. It just means you may be drawing on a cache of willpower that will be less than full.

Taking action early in the day is a suggestion. It's not a requirement. If it doesn't apply to your activity, don't worry about it. Do your activity when it makes sense for you.

Do Celebrate, Don't Reward

Traditional goal-setting is a paradigm of work/reward. "If I do this, then later I get that." For big goals, we have already discussed how ineffective this approach is for the 80%-er. Using the micro-version to try to develop behavior is also problematic.

For example, "If I recruit a new distributor, then I treat myself to a spa day." The first issue is that you are rewarding yourself. How exciting can that be? Assuming you have the money, what's the big deal? You can afford a spa day now. You can afford a spa day a month from now. Where's the motivational juice in that?

We replaced traditional goals with "ER" directions. Let's replace rewards with celebrations. People desperately want recognition and appreciation. Let's give that gift to ourselves. For the 80%, this is that instant gratification fix that we desire. Take a moment. Enjoy the accomplishment. Really feel the victory.

It's great when other people express their respect for us. It's even better when we earn it from ourselves.

George—*Every day that I worked out, I celebrated. It wasn't a big deal. Upon completion of my Chain activity, I simply looked in the mirror and congratulated myself. I allowed myself to feel* *proud. Really feel it. In all honesty, that's what I craved more than anything else. I wanted to know I had done my best that day. That sense of being in control of myself and my life, one day at a time, was much more inspiring than the thought of getting some new toy at the end of the month.*

The Power of Positive Direction

There are two types of possible Chain activities: positive and negative. The difference is simple. Positive activities require us to <u>do</u> something. Negative activities require us to <u>not</u> do something.

We've focused primarily on the positive.

For example, "I'm going to introduce my opportunity to one new person a day." A negative activity would be something similar to, "I'm not going to smoke a cigarette today."

While the authors would love all our readers to enjoy a healthy, smoke-free life, that may not be the best Chain to start with. First, these kinds of Chains come with a very high degree of difficulty. Some even require physical and psychological withdrawal. That may be more that you want to tackle with the first Chain. Second, until the clock strikes 11:59:59, you can't claim victory. That leaves very little time to celebrate.

Chapter 17

The World Ain't Fair

Despite your best efforts, things can happen. No matter how much we plan and how hard we try, stuff goes wrong.

Your Chain may break.

Now what? The typical 80% response would be to berate ourselves and feel like a failure. However, if you have built a Chain long enough to engender that kind of an emotional response, there is another option.

How long was the Chain? Two weeks? One month? Three months?

Ask yourself, "Before I tried this Consistency Chain technique, how many days in a row did I perform consistently?" Maybe two or three? Probably one. Even more probably, none. Look at the days marked off on your calendar. You don't have to feel bad. You can feel proud. However many days your Chain is, it almost certainly beat your old, inconsistent track record.

Go to the calendar. Go to your app. Take notice of your record. Now here is the most important action you will ever take: Start again. Today. Don't wait until Monday. Don't take the weekend off. Start today. Momentum is powerful, but it's not indestructible. Don't take a chance on it slipping away. Put a new link on the board. Pick up the Chain. The good news is that now you have a target. Build this Chain longer than the last.

Jim—In building a health Chain, I have come to understand the difference between "falling off the wagon" and being pushed. Falling off the wagon is just nonchalantly breaking the Chain. Being "pushed" is when outside circumstances make daily action impossible. Prior to using the Consistency Chain approach, I could go weeks with no vigorous physical activity. It was absolutely no big deal. In fact, I wouldn't even notice.

However, once I was a few months into building my health and fitness Chain, things were different. I had to have minor surgery.

George—*Implants?*

Jim—Cut it out. While the procedure was minimal, the doctor told me that I couldn't have any sort of physical exertion for a week. All of a sudden, not being able to take my daily walk was a huge deal. I experienced "Chain withdrawal." I had a real desire to work out. And the day my doctor gave me permission to return to my Chain is the day that I began again.

Understand that if you can do these three things, you can have or be virtually anything that you want.

1) Start your Chain today.
2) If the worst happens and the Chain breaks, just congratulate yourself for the effort that went into that Chain.
3) And without delay, start the Chain again. Today.

If you can do those three things, you are unstoppable.

Jim—It's unfair. It takes months to create momentum and days to lose it. My rule is simple (unless a doctor is involved): Never miss two days in a row. One day is an accident. Two days is a trend. Three days is something from which you may never recover.

Start a "Chain Gang"

This is the final recommendation to lock in your success. When you combine "peer-to-peer" support (the Chain Gang) with the simplicity of the Consistency Chain, the results are astounding. Understand, this is not an absolutely required step. Jim and George built their first Chains without this system. But why would you not take advantage of this unbelievably powerful tool?

__Jim__—I see you're trying to cut down that tree with a butter knife. Could I interest you in a chainsaw?

A Chain Gang is a manageably small group of accountability partners. These are people who are on the same consistency journey as you. They don't have to live near you or work with you. They don't have to be involved in the same Chain activity as you. You don't even need to know the details of their activity. Everyone just has to be willing to share their daily Consistency Chain victories and support the others in theirs.

The ultimate goal is to be accountable to ourselves. But, until we are strong enough to accomplish that, like-minded partners can be a crucial difference maker. It's a sad truth that sometimes we are more likely to keep promises to others, than we are to ourselves.

__George__—My first real Chain was started several years ago. And I didn't know I was even doing it. I began a project with my 20% best friend. We are both business humorists. For years, other professional speakers had asked us to share advice, tips and guidance on how to add more humor to their programs.

We decided we would formalize our accumulated knowledge and experience into a humor course called FunnierU.com. As part of that program, we would provide speakers, sales trainers, and salespeople with daily topical humor. This meant that my partner and I would write five jokes apiece, five days a week. Of those ten daily jokes, we would select the three best to go out to our subscribers every workday morning.

That began over eight years ago. In that span of time, neither my partner nor I have ever missed a single day of turning in our work. This regimen forced me to be more consistent and prolific than I had ever been. Each of us has written over 12,000 jokes.

The reason for this perfect participation is simple. He is not going to let me down. I am not going to let him down. My partner and I are accountable to each other as business partners and as best friends.

Imagine adding supportive accountability partners to the already powerful Consistency Chain concept (the word "unstoppable" comes to mind).

Jim—*When I was a young man selling copiers for SCM Corp., I developed my first weekly accountability form. I would not go back to the office without having visited one prospective customer and finding out what kind of copier they were currently using. I wasn't selling them a copier—I was just taking the first step that could lead to a sale. In network marketing, when you reach out and connect with someone, you aren't recruiting them. You are just taking the first step that may lead to them joining your business as a distributor or customer. This simple Chain activity, resulted in my always being in the company's top 10 sales reps, with over 600 reps in the country.*

When I was building my network marketing business, I averaged one product demonstration per day. This simple action resulted in me being the all-time leader in enrollments.

I had my sons, Jeff and Adam, as accountability partners. We were constantly holding each other accountable. That is partly the reason, at one network marketing company, all three of us were among the top 10 income earners for over 10 years. Ralph Waldo Emerson said we need someone to make us do the things we're capable of doing. My sons certainly did that for me.

Positive accountability is the ultimate "Win-Win" relationship. My sons were the first distributors that I enrolled. They achieved Distributor and Runner-up Distributor of the Year respectively! (That's me being a proud father, sorry.)

Keep in mind a couple of ideas on accountability. There is a fine line between collaboration and competition.

For some, the idea of competing is very attractive and energizing. The problem with competition is that, by definition, there is going to be a winner and a loser. That means someone could build a very impressive Chain, lose a "competition," and still feel bad about it. The other aspect to competition is that there is a stopping point. (Other than a cricket match, which apparently lasts forever.) The entire point of the Consistency Chain is not to "win" but to change. Our victory is gaining control over our lives and actions. There is no post-game celebration to this. It is an ongoing, daily winning streak.

Collaboration is people committing to support and encourage each other in a combined endeavor. Collaboration is not having someone to race; it's having a running buddy.

Setting Up a Chain Gang:

There are five simple steps for setting up a "Consistency Chain Gang":

1) Find 3-5 people who want to build a Consistency Chain.

2) Set up a group text. (If you don't know how to do this, ask your kids.)

3) Each day, when you complete your task, simply let the group know.

4) As the others chime in, congratulations are in order. (Emojis are perfect for this.)

5) As the day draws to a close, check for stragglers, and send encouragement their way.

George—*I was wrestling with my third Chain. My Chain activity was—for me—a very challenging mental exercise. Percentage-wise, I was winning more often than not, but I was far from consistent. Jim and I had discussed the power of accountability, but we had never really put it into practice. We decided to put accountability to the test with the very first Chain Gang. The result? The gaps in our Chains disappeared immediately. After a month, we expanded the test and added another "gangsta" to our group. Jim enlisted a woman who had just read the book and wanted to start her Chain. After another 100 days, we added two more to our gang.*

Jim—*Let me finish the story. Since day one, our Chain Gang has had 100% success, 100% of the time. That includes those people who were brand new to the Chain concept. They were fighting through the most challenging time, the initial beginning of a Chain. Yet, every single person won the day, every single day.*

Part of the power of the Chain Gang is those unpredictable "pings" you get throughout the day. Sometimes, people have the best of intentions to accomplish their Chain activity, but they simply forget. With a Chain Gang, that isn't possible.

Before you reject this on the grounds of "busyness," consider that being fully engaged in this kind of group usually requires less than five minutes a day. And, we have a TON of fun in our gang, and we encourage you to do the same. As George always reminds me, "This is too important to be taken seriously."

The last thought on accountability is this: Don't wait to start if you don't have an accountability partner.

George—*We almost didn't add the "accountability" section to the book for this very reason. I know me (80%-er). I know I will jump on any excuse to avoid taking action. "Gosh, those guys said accountability is really important, but I don't have anybody. Maybe I should just wait until those people show up at my door."*

Having accountability partners is great. It's helpful. But <u>please</u> *understand this: It's not required. What is required is that you START! Right now! Today!*

BTW, you really do have an accountability partner. Yourself. That is the most important person to whom you have to be responsible. Don't wait. Start!

Jim—*I just realized that by writing this book, we have made ourselves accountable to everyone who reads it. No pressure there.*

Chapter 18

Last Words

George—*If there is anything special about me, it would be this: I never gave up searching.*

Despite endless disappointment and lack of results, I always believed I would find something that would turn it around. Or more to the point, turn me around.

I didn't want my epitaph to read, "Great potential, mediocre results." It wasn't like I was a failure before. I always got by. It's just that I wanted a life of more than merely "getting by." I wanted a life I could be proud of. So, I kept looking.

No one is more surprised than me that my personal epiphany revolves around an 18th century Italian and a 20th century comedian.

If you're an 80%-er like me, you've probably had people tell you, "You can do it!" Then to their frustration and yours, you didn't do it. I'm not going to tell you that you can do it. I'm simply going to say that you can do THIS.

I turned myself from inconsistent to consistent to constant. There was no magic. I just won Day Three. You can do that.

Jim—*It's interesting how both George and I stumbled across this method years ago and didn't realize what it was or why it worked.*

When I was building my copier business, we reached a critical crossroads at about year 10. Our debt to equity ratio was 35 to 1, and we were drowning in red ink. We were so desperate that we went to our competitors to see if they would just buy us out and give us jobs. No one was willing to absorb our debt. That experience was very humbling to say the least.

I remember the day my partner and I were sitting at Fuddruckers discussing our options. My partner laughingly suggested we should "make" all of the salespeople "do what you do every day!" Not to brag, but we had seven salespeople at that time, and I would consistently outsell them all every month combined.

Most people would attribute this to the fact that I owned the company had the best prospects. The truth of the matter was I was utilizing the Consistency Chain back then. I just didn't call it that. My success originated in the fact that I isolated one key sales driving activity and made sure that I did it every day.

We started a "daily" accountability program that turned our company around. We helped our associates focus on that key activity and tracked their daily efforts. That's how we went on to become the 22nd largest Sharp dealership in the country, out of over 600.

This ranking was achieved despite the fact we were located in sparsely populated Maine. When we sold our business to a Fortune 500 company, we were told our sales per employee was in the top 1% for all copier companies.

And to echo George, if there was anything special about me, it would be my love of personal growth. I never want to be too old to learn and grow. Because of the opportunity to share this Consistency Chain idea, I have a new lease on life. I am energized by the possibility of helping thousands of people.

In fairness, that has been my mission for years. But, in the past, the results of my efforts have not been as effective as I'd hoped. I kept sharing my 20% strategies with 80% people. And nothing would change.

George says it is very hard to lead people who you don't understand. Now I do understand. Now I am even more committed to helping people make a better life for themselves and their family.

I have had a saying on my desk for years that reads, "I Live in the Place that I Belong, with the People that I Love, doing the Right work on Purpose." Until recently, I questioned what that right work was. I don't anymore.

Decide.

Start.

Don't break the Chain.

Thank you for reading The Consistency Chain for Network Marketing!

If you would like to fast-track your future, we have a valuable offer. Go to:

ConsistencyChain.com/coaching

and sign up for a free one hour consultation with one of our trained, certified coaches. Let them help you get started. Then you can decide if their ongoing help would be valuable to you. Several tiers of coaching are available, all the way up to daily interaction with the authors, Jim and George.

While you are on our website, don't forget to go and download the free Consistency Chain App!

Our goal is to impact as many people in the world of network marketing as possible. As *The Consistency Chain* strategy works for you, please let your upline leaders know!

And, if you've enjoyed reading this book, we would deeply appreciate an honest review of the book on the buying platform of your choice.

Printed in Great Britain
by Amazon

44617715R00068